THE TIMES

careers & jobs
in the
media

simon kent

KOGAN
PAGE

First published in Great Britain in 2005

Kogan Page Limited
120 Pentonville Road
London N1 9JN
United Kingdom
www.kogan-page.co.uk

© Simon Kent, 2005

British Library Cataloguing in Publication Data

A CIP record for this book is available from the British Library.

ISBN 0 7494 4247 6

Typeset by Saxon Graphics Ltd, Derby
Printed and bound in Great Britain by Creative Print and Design (Wales), Ebbw Vale

Contents

Introduction   **1**

1. **Journalism**   **5**
    The structure of the industry, Occupational areas,
    Allied professions, Getting started

2. **Publishing**   **17**
    The structure of the industry, Occupational areas,
    Allied professions, Getting started

3. **Broadcast media: television**   **31**
    The structure of the industry, Occupational areas,
    Allied professions, Getting started

4. **Broadcast media: radio**   **47**
    The structure of the industry, Occupational areas,
    Allied professions, Getting started

5. **Film**   **59**
    The structure of the industry, Occupational areas,
    Allied professions, Getting started

6. **New media**   **71**
    The structure of the industry, Occupational areas,
    Allied professions, Getting started

7. Top tips 85

8. Self-assessment tests and questionnaires 87
English as she is written, Reasonable logic, Yet
more logic, Logical practice, Answers to tests

9. Frequently asked questions 95

10. Where to study 101
Do I need to study at all?, What kind of course?,
Computer packages to know and learn,
Media courses

11. Useful addresses 117
Unions, professional associations and interest
groups; Employers; Recruitment

Index 123

Introduction

IS THIS THE JOB FOR YOU?

Ten things to ask yourself when considering a job in the media

- Do you have an insatiable appetite for knowledge, facts and stories?

- Are you obsessed with film, television, current affairs, radio or the internet?

- Can you think of new, creative and innovative ideas for the media?

- Do you want to influence the opinions and activities of the rest of the country?

- Are you able to keep your cool under pressure?

- Are you willing to work extraordinarily long hours?

- Can you work in collaboration with others?

- Have you got the confidence to challenge those in power?

- Are you willing to travel anywhere and everywhere for a good job or a great story?

- Do you want to work at the cutting edge of entertainment and information technology?

1

INTRODUCTION

It is impossible to put an exact figure on the size of the media industry, in terms of either the turnover created by the sector or the number of people employed. Sources suggest that on the print side of the industry alone there are over 3,500 book publishers in the UK, 9,000 magazine titles, 30 national newspaper titles and close to 2,000 local and online-based news reporting organisations. We can add to this some 24,000 people working in broadcast television, 23,000 in radio and thousands more working in new media, both within dedicated independent new media companies and within more traditional media organisations.

The media is all-pervasive. It affects, influences, reflects and analyses every aspect of our lives. It generates enormous pleasure, hatred, envy, joy – you name it. A news report can save the lives of some people, destroy the lives of others. The importance of the media is not just that the news service tells us what's happening or gives us a chance to ask questions of people in power, but that the people who control and operate in the media are often able to determine wider events and trends, nationally and internationally.

In the past year or more the Iraq War and surrounding political fall-out has dominated the news. But it has not simply been the politician's actions under the spotlight – the death of David Kelly, consequent investigations and the eventual ousting of Greg Dyke, Director-General of the BBC, raised serious questions about the role and responsibilities of journalists in creating and reporting news stories. Interestingly, one result of the Hutton enquiry appears to be that the BBC will be establishing its own journalism training school in the future.

Never mind factual events, in the past year huge blockbusting films have dictated aspects of our everyday life. *Harry Potter* – together with its original series of books – has not simply entertained a generation of readers, but created an entire world in which young people can submerge themselves. Across the country and across the world shelves are stacked with Harry Potter merchandise, Harry Potter computer games. The same is true of *The Lord of The Rings* and *The Matrix*. This isn't just entertainment – it's a lifestyle.

As I write, summer is upon us and already thousands of young clubbers are out in Ibiza, the summer home of club culture. Without the influence of the media – from radio broadcasts to newspapers, magazine coverage and extensive promotional websites – such an event would not exist. The media is not just a global phenomenon; it creates global phenomena. It does not just make the world a smaller place; it makes it easy for ideas, cultures and activities to be shared around the world in the fastest possible time.

You don't need me to tell you how important the media is to you already – before you've even set out to make a living from the industry. Not a day goes by without you or everyone you know being influenced in some way by the media or engaging with a product created by a media company. Turn on the radio or television, flick through a book or magazine, and already you are engaged with the industry. Count the number of times you go on the internet with your computer, dial up an interactive site with your mobile phone or sit down in front of the silver screen to watch the latest movies or rent the recent releases from the library or video hire shop: the media is a critical part of life, keeping us informed, educated and entertained in equal measure.

So it must be a great place to work, right? Well, yes and no. Certainly the opportunities exist to really make your name in the media world, either as a celebrity creative (a DJ, presenter, journalist, author) or as an effective part of management, creating the right environment and securing the necessary funding for the creative talents of others to truly flourish. However, this is an unforgiving and tough industry. It rewards those who make the right connections, deliver the right products at the right time and to the right budget. It severely punishes those who have not quite thought through their plan – those who do not quite meet the requirements of the contemporary audience and those who do not appear to use the media with integrity and honour.

There are a few basic ground rules to bear in mind when approaching the media as a workplace and finding your ideal employer. First, determination and enthusiasm is everything. It is not enough to do an OK or competent job – you must deliver at 100 per cent of your ability every time. In your early career you will have no experience and no track record – enthusiasm is the only thing you have.

Second, always be ready with fresh ideas and innovative thinking. The media does not stand still for very long. What makes the headlines of today wraps up the fish and chips of tomorrow, and the same is true across all media. A website, novel, film, television or radio programme may tap into the zeitgeist of today but tomorrow no one will be interested. If you are planning to be anything creative in the media you must be ready to move on as tastes change. Anticipate the next big thing, discover new talent before anyone else does – and don't under any circumstances continue to do the same job in the same way and expect it always to bring you success.

The aspects that make life in the media exciting are the same aspects that make life in the media hard. You can never really rest on your laurels. The public's appetite for something new, exciting and immediate is the only constant thing you will have in your working life. The following pages will show you how to tap into that appetite, how to get yourself into the fast-flowing media stream, how to survive and how to succeed.

1

Journalism

THE STRUCTURE OF THE INDUSTRY

Recent years have seen radical changes in the working lives of journalists. Large print media organisations – both newspapers and magazines – have undergone restructuring as they have adapted to the increased presence and popularity of electronic media: the internet, interactive television and so on. The number of broadsheet newspapers has reduced, and the number of full-time positions on publications has fallen as companies have sought to reduce costs. At the same time there has been an expansion of smaller independent publications in some areas of magazine publishing. Both these trends have resulted in an expansion of opportunities for freelance writers – although these opportunities are by no means always very lucrative.

Computer packages have brought the tools required to create a publication to a larger number of people, and reduced the initial cost required to start up a new publication. Desktop publishing systems such as Quark XPress allow skilled operators to lay out pages professionally and save them in a format a printing company can use. Combine this with an internet site through which interested readers can be attracted and made to part with their subscription money, and the result is that anyone can create a publication which can be mailed out and read by thousands of people.

The major employers of journalists – broadsheet papers, broadcasting companies and so on – are easy to find and approach for work. Go down to your local newsagent and scan the shelves of newspapers and magazines, and you will soon see the wealth of subjects now covered in print. Flick through the first few pages and you will find the contents list, perhaps a note from the editor and, most importantly, details of the company behind the publication – the publisher.

In the case of the daily papers, publications such as the *Guardian*, the *Daily Telegraph*, *The Times*, the *Daily Mail* and so on are part of larger companies which have grown around their news-stand presence. Each company has other publishing concerns, most notably internet sites which complement or are in addition to the daily printed copy. These publications reflect and influence the concerns of the country on a day-by-day, week-by-week basis. In order to be successful, newspapers must select and present the news – both national and international issues, events and politics – in a way that will appeal to their readership. As such, most newspapers carry some kind of political bias (the *Guardian* is more left-wing, the *Telegraph* more right-wing and so on). Newspapers also carry supplements covering specific areas of interest – the arts, motoring, style, society and so on. Again, journalists on these titles seek to reflect and affect the thinking and opinions of readers on a national basis.

Flick through the magazines, and you will find there are a few major companies running a range of titles. Emap – publishers of *Heat, Q Magazine* and *New Woman* – also runs a business-to-business publishing service and works in radio and television. IPC publishes magazines from *Woman's Own* to *Loaded* to *Cage and Aviary Birds*. Magazines split into two types: 'consumer' publications, of interest to the general public (that is, lifestyle magazines) and 'trade' publications which provide news, views and information relating to professional matters, dealing with workplace specialisms such as grocery store owners and generic functions such as management or medical jobs. Like the broadsheet and tabloid newspapers, the magazines you see on the shelves have a national readership, and sometimes even have international readers or sister titles supplying readers in other countries. Titles such as *GQ* and *Vogue* are published in America and France, and some trade publications also stray across national boundaries.

In addition to these magazines, you will also find there are local publications – newspapers which have small offices local to the geographical areas they cover. These papers reflect the concerns of the neighbourhoods they represent. They may cover local politics, charity works, events and so on. Occasionally they may run a story which has national significance, but this is usually a result of chance, because one of the national newspapers has picked up on the story, rather than because the local press has reported it. These publications are sometimes distributed free to residents in the area they cover.

Finally there are some publications that you will not see in your local newsagents. These are specialist or corporate magazines produced by publishers for very specific readers. Specialist magazines are delivered by post to subscribers who pay for them on a regular basis. These magazines may cover very specific subjects – model making, leisure interests and so on – or they may be more academic, covering analysis of new poetry, the latest developments in technology and so on. The fact is, because the readers are so specific and sometimes so few, there is little point in putting the publication on a newsagent's shelf – it simply is not worth using up that space.

Corporate publications or 'in-house' magazines are produced by large employers as a means of telling their employees what is going on in the company on a regular basis. These publications sometimes use dedicated journalists whose job it is to collect stories from around the company, talk to the people involved and create a readable magazine for the entire company. This practice is sometimes known as 'contract publishing'.

In all print media it is rare – if not impossible – to find a publication that makes money purely through its cover price. Instead, the print media makes money through advertisers. Advertisers will buy space in the publication, paying an amount appropriate to the profile of the publication and how many people read the magazine. For this reason it costs less to advertise in a local newspaper then it does a national publication.

BEFORE YOU START GOING ANYWHERE IN JOURNALISM

Since there are diverse workplaces for journalists it is important that you should decide what type of journalist you want to be from the very start:

- Do you want to write about news and current affairs, trends and fashion or historical events and research?

- Do you have particular knowledge about an area of leisure, such as music, video games, business or IT?

- Do you want to write for a national readership and influence the topic of debate among your readers?

- How close do you want to be to your readers? Local press and corporate publications usually mean being a part of that community; national publications have a greater distance. In both cases you are bound to receive prompt (and not always favourable) feedback for what you write. If you are writing for a high-profile national publication, you may find your writing is subject to greater criticism and/or serious analysis by those you are writing about and for. On the other hand, get your facts wrong or misquote someone in a local newspaper, and he or she might never talk to you again.

Contract to publish

With a career lasting over 25 years, John Wisbey has moved from news-stand journalism to strategic business consulting to founding and directing Publicis Blueprint – a contract publisher creating magazines, web content and other material for business clients. 'With news-stand publishing, there's a two-way relationship between yourself and your readers,' he says. 'You have to identify what it is your readers want and make sure they're satisfied. With contract publishing there's more of a triangle. You need to engage with the readers, but you also need to engage with the brand. There's still the challenge of making people read your publication – because you can't force someone to read something – but the job of contract publishing is to understand what the brand message is and find an engaging way to say that too.'

Publicis Blueprint employs editors, designers, account managers, sales people, planners and production staff. Wisbey is adamant that in each discipline it is important that the individual demonstrates absolute passion for their subject and for the overall importance of publishing to deliver messages to readers effectively and entertainingly. Anyone who demonstrates an understanding of the way to grow the business – expanding through new clients or increasing the publications delivered to existing clients – will find his or her work rewarded and will rise through the ranks.

Wisbey began his career in a media sales role and notes that this is a very good area to begin your career because it immediately gives you an overview on the business of publishing and the strategy that lies behind successful publications. It is possible to cross from media sales to a more creative role, and the ability to understand and work with external clients will always be a plus for any employee.

'You've got to be a team player to succeed in this business,' adds Wisbey. 'That's not to say we don't look for high-performing individuals, but if you can't work alongside everyone else then you're not going to be as effective as someone who can.'

OCCUPATIONAL AREAS

Since publications vary dramatically in size, readership and budget, the number of these staff in any given publication will also vary. A national newspaper may have dozens of reporters, several section editors and so on. A specialist publication may be run by a single editor who writes material, commissions and sub-edits articles from other writers.

Reporters

Within newspapers and larger publications, reporters are usually attached to specific sections – news and current affairs, politics, the arts, finance, money and so on. Reporters may be mobile, travelling around the country and even the world in order to cover news stories. They may find themselves being given ongoing assignments in specific geographic locations, or simply being asked to cover a single event. Other reporters may have desk jobs, where most of their information comes via the phone, posted reports, leads from other sources and so on.

Reporters often work unsociable hours. A story can break any time of the day or night. A career in journalism may also dictate the type of people you know and the places you visit. If you are a business journalist working on a trade publication, for example, you will need to attend conferences, seminars, lunches and even the occasional party in order to make good contacts within your subject area. You will therefore need to get on well with the people who work in the industry you cover in order to be sure you always know what's going on.

Sub-editors

It is the sub-editor's job to make sure that an article submitted to a publication reads well, makes sense and conforms to the publication's style. Since articles may come from a number of different writers, if the pieces went straight into print the reader might find it difficult to read from page to page. By standardising the articles, there is a greater chance that everything in the publication will be read. Sub-editors need to be very astute and thorough, able to spot grammatical errors and to correct those errors without distorting the reporter's intentions.

Editors

The direction and contents of every publication are ultimately the responsibility of the editor. He or she has overall control of what gets written and what does not. In a busy newspaper office the editor may hold regular editorial meetings during which reporters or section editors can pitch their ideas for stories. The editor will decide which stories are the ones to follow up and feature in depth, and allocate work among the reporters to get those stories written. He or she might decide, for example, that one story is so important that it is worth having the news reporters do a substantial article on the subject, and find a specialist reporter to do a piece that illustrates another aspect of this story. For instance, a headline-grabbing crime might be covered by the news staff, by a regional reporter and by a legal/crime specialist.

On daily publications the editor will work to a number of deadlines throughout the day, leading up to the actual print run which occurs every night. In a weekly, monthly, bi-monthly or quarterly publication the deadlines worked to will be a little longer, but there will still be the last-minute dash to get everything ready for press day. It is also likely on these longer-run publications that the editor will have to work several weeks and even months in advance in order to organise the writing and submission of articles. Trade publications, for example, will know what subjects they will cover for the next year or so, partly so the advertising sales staff can sell space in the magazine against those articles.

Photographers

Photojournalists are given specific assignments to produce the images that go alongside the written words. This can include attending newsworthy events – sports activities, visits of important people, even capturing images of war or disaster. Alternatively, they might be asked to shoot products for a consumer magazine – pictures of new technology, clothes, accessories and so on. For trade publications they might need to arrange a shooting session with the subject of an interview or a writer who has contributed to the magazine. 'Paparazzi' photographers make their money by taking and selling candid shots of celebrities, frequently caught off their guard. Photojournalists' work can be more serious and provocative. Some have earned a great reputation and have even been exhibited in art galleries.

Layout and design

While the usual image of a worker on a newspaper or magazine is a reporter with a notebook or photographer with a camera, it should not be forgotten that someone needs to be employed to put all of this material together on the printed page. Layout and design staff are responsible for the overall style and look of the magazine. They ensure that the text is legible, that it fits on the page, and that images used make the maximum impact. They may also be on hand to create advertisements for the publication. According to the size of the publication there might be dedicated designers to do this, or the task might be carried out by the sub-editors.

Freelance journalists

The use of freelance workers has increased dramatically in recent years. The availability of suitable technology, e-mail and access to the internet has meant that publications can receive articles written by people all over the country – and all over the world – direct into their own systems, and from there transfer them onto the printed page. Moreover, by farming work out to freelancers, organisations have been able to cut their operating costs.

If you want to set yourself up as a freelance writer you will need to get in touch with the editors of the publications you want to write for. If editors know who you are and what you can write about, they might commission you, giving you a deadline by which time they should receive the piece, the length of the article, and how much they will pay you.

Freelancers have to be ready to pitch ideas to the publication's editor, either verbally over the phone or in writing via e-mail or letter. They need to tell the editor why he or she should use the idea, and why they are the best person to write the piece. Many photographers are also freelancers, and work to a similar structure, taking on assignments given to them by editors, or offering photos they think a publication will be interested in.

ALLIED PROFESSIONS

Since journalists are skilled at finding out information and presenting it in a way that can be understood and appreciated by many others, they can find work in diverse organisations that deal with information.

Research

People with journalistic skills can work with research organisations in the preparation of reports and documents. They may carry out specific research projects themselves for private clients, perhaps into the kind of competition a company has or into future trends among a company's customers.

Cross-media work

With the increase in different kinds of media – television, the internet and so on – many journalists aim to get skills which mean they can report in sound and vision as well as words.

PR and communications

Journalists have also been known to 'switch sides' and work in press offices and PR agencies – companies where the emphasis is on getting a story into the press. With their direct experience of the press, journalists can approach editors in the most effective way. They can create concise press releases, coordinate interviews with spokespeople, and even contribute quotes themselves. In some cases they might even write articles to promote the goods and services of their clients.

Author! Author!

Some journalists have become book writers, either using their knowledge to write factual books on specific subjects, or creating works of fiction based on their observations of the world around them.

Hands on

Finally, it is not unknown for journalists to make the leap from writing about their subject to actually doing something in their subject area. Having got to know their subject in depth, they may feel they can contribute in a real way to that business. One former editor of *Smash Hits* magazine went on to have a very successful pop-star career. Many business writers find their way into business consultancy, either giving their insight into business trends for the good of their clients, or becoming management gurus/experts themselves.

GETTING STARTED

The traditional way into the print media still exists. This is an apprenticeship model, which means starting as a 'cub reporter' (that is, a junior reporter, not someone who reports on cubs) at a small local newspaper. In this role you will get to know how the paper works. You will see how the paper delivers copy to the printers to strict deadlines, how the reporters and editor coordinate their work, and how the sales staff operate. Eventually you will be given some writing work and encouraged to develop new reporting skills. When you feel you are ready and have enough experience, you can move on to a more senior reporting position, and work your way up the industry, taking on more responsibility and working on higher-profile stories and higher-profile publications.

That said, it is far more usual now for journalists to get into the industry after some kind of vocational training. The fact is that there is such high competition for places in the industry that publishers can select the people they want, and take on only those who have demonstrated, through experience or at least a portfolio of work, that they have the skills required.

There is another route into the industry which does not require a vocational degree. If you go to college and take a qualification in a completely unrelated subject, you can still develop your journalistic skills by working on a student publication. Most colleges publish a weekly newspaper which features reviews, news and opinions about student life. If you play a part in that, you can get student membership of the National Union of Journalists and really kick-start your career.

Alternatively, you can specialise in a very definite subject area, again unrelated to journalism. If you present yourself well, your specialist knowledge will make you very attractive to editors and publishers who want to feature cutting-edge knowledge and views from professionals. If you study history, for example, you may be able to offer a specialist article on a certain period of history you have researched.

Whatever area of the press you want to get involved in, you must be ready to demonstrate your skills. Even if no one is paying you for your work, you must write and keep on writing – anything and everything – so you are used to staring at a blank computer screen or piece of paper and filling it with words. If you want to be a photojournalist, keep taking photos – anywhere and everywhere. Unless you train yourself to create something out of nothing and do it to a deadline, you will never convince an editor that he or she should take you on.

Type cast

Dan Nelson works for a local paper in a northern English town. He always wanted to be a journalist, and just asked the paper if it would take him on for work experience during the school holidays. Once he had completed his A levels, the paper gave him his first job. 'When you first think of working in print journalism you have this image of going in at the top – being the investigative reporter who discovers some incredible story,' he says. 'But to be honest you quickly realise how little you really know.'

Nelson has learnt a lot about working to deadlines, finding stories, and what makes people read the paper. 'We have a very lively postbag and some fairly irate people write in regularly,' he says. 'It doesn't completely dictate what we include in the paper, but if you want to get the circulation up you begin to realise what you need to do.'

Since the paper is fairly small and local, Nelson has worked on just about every page. 'I've reviewed films, been to school fetes, attended police press conferences – you name it, I've done it. I was particularly proud when I had my first front cover story,' he says, 'Although now it's happened a few times it's become a bit run of the mill.'

As for the future, Nelson is hopeful for a break into the national press. 'I've got a couple of options for my career,' he says. 'I could stay in the local press and work my way up – there's the chance of getting to editor level within this sector, and what you don't realise is that a lot of the regional papers are owned by the same company. That means you can get promotion to other titles within the company rather than having to start from scratch with a new editor every time.'

'I still want to get into the nationals,' he continues. 'I'm trying to establish myself as a good regional reporter – if something important happens around here, I want to be the person they come to for the details. Whether I can do that full-time or as a freelancer I'm not sure – but at the moment I just need to keep finding the exciting stories and cover them as best I can.'

2

Publishing

THE STRUCTURE OF THE INDUSTRY

The growth of the internet and other electronically based media has undoubtedly had an impact on the publishing industry. However, the printed page is still alive and healthy, and it seems certain that no matter how much of our lives is transferred online, there will always be a place for the printed word. Whether it is a paperback novel, a coffee table photography book or an educational resource, a book delivers information in a format which is unique and necessary. Entertainment and education will always occur through the printed page.

That said, it should be noted that book publishing is a challenging industry to enter and in which to build a career. There are a limited number of companies working in this field, and the trend has been to employ fewer staff and get as much work as possible carried out by freelancers. According to one source the majority of publishing companies employ only 10–12 people.

Book publishers usually specialise in a particular market place. There are children and young people's titles carried by companies such as Dorling Kindersley, fiction houses, including the large publishers such as Random House and Penguin, and academic publishers such as the Oxford University Press. What you may not realise is that many publishing names are actually owned by the bigger publishing houses. Penguin, for example, publishes Puffin books and also owns the Rough Guide titles. Even large companies break down their publishing activities into smaller departments, recognising how important it is that readers should be able to associate each publisher's identity with the type of book produced.

Popular publishing – the writing, creation and marketing of novels – still remains a lucrative area for publishers. Everyone wants to find the next Booker Prize winner, the next blockbusting story and the next genre of story to capture the public's imagination. Popular fiction is responsive to contemporary fashions and trends. In 1996 Picador published a book called *Bridget Jones's Diary* by Helen Fielding – a fun but reasonably straightforward first-person account of a young woman's attempt to conform to the perfect image of womanhood and to get herself a boyfriend. Not only did the novel lead to a successful film, it also triggered a number of other 'chick lit' publications – stories told by women about the ordeals of being a career woman, and an attractive person with or without a love interest.

The incredible popularity of *Harry Potter* has created a great interest in children's and young people's fiction. *Harry Potter* also demonstrates the importance of considering other media when dealing in publishing. If you can sign up a writer whose work is then optioned by a film company, that means extra revenue for the publisher. If the film then actually gets made – by no means a certainty – not only will the publisher make yet more revenue from the film, it will also be able to sell more books to an extended audience.

Other useful tie-ins which publishers should be aware of are computer games, merchandise and complementary publications. The latter are 'spin-off' books which might or might not be written by the original author, but which further explore elements of that book or the world the author has created. (See *Quidditch Through the Ages* and other *Harry Potter* guides.)

If the publisher cannot get a film made out of the book, it might be able to get a newspaper to publish passages from it as a 'taster' of the publication. For important, well-known and best-selling authors some newspapers will publish extracts or even serialise the whole book within their pages. While a complete serialisation might seem likely to reduce the number of people who would want to buy the book, it actually has the reverse effect – after all, the newspaper will probably get thrown away in the end, so if readers like the book and want to own it, they will have to go out and buy it.

Finally, you know you have reached publishing heaven when a book is so popular that its readers are clamouring for a sequel. Again, *Harry Potter* has proved the apex of this phenomenon – the next volume is even an important event for adult readers. However, sequels are also important if an author has created an attractive detective, hero or villain. Again, identifying and publishing these kinds of books spells publishing success.

While the internet and IT may not have signalled the death of traditional publishing, technology has altered the nature of the industry. As in the newspaper industry, the number of skilled and dedicated workers now required on the production side of the industry has diminished. It is now possible to write, lay out and design a large book on a single desktop computer, creating the finished article in a format ready to go to the printer.

The internet has placed the onus on books to be more interactive, more challenging and involving. On one level this affects the style and content of books – the emphasis sometimes moves to more impressive visuals which cannot be reproduced to the same quality through a computer screen. However, there has also been technology developed which offers 3D images for children's books and interactive pages which enable viewers or readers to find out more about the subject they are studying in the same way that clicking on a link on a web page can take you to more detailed information.

BEFORE YOU GO ANYWHERE IN PUBLISHING

- What area of publishing do you want to go into? Academic, popular, children's or more specialist? You must be certain about this because you need to know your market, know the publishers in this area, and know the most important and popular authors and titles.

- Do you want to work on production, marketing or editorial? Again, each of these areas requires different skills, and you should tailor the early stages of your career to reflect these differences.

- Get a feel for current trends within the publishing industry. Don't just look at what is being promoted on the bookshelves; buy the industry press and find out exactly how many copies are being sold. Find out how the marketing campaigns are handled and who is identifying whom as the next big thing in publishing.

- Keep an eye on the sellers. Books are now being sold through websites as well as on the high street – indeed, there's a swift trade occurring online for second-hand books. Know how this will affect the industry.

OCCUPATIONAL AREAS

Author

Some large educational and business publishers employ full-time writers who can deliver high-quality copy on a daily basis. However, the majority of authors are self-employed – holed up in their garret or bedroom, striving to get their manuscript finished, hoping that someone will read it and decide it is good enough for a wider audience.

Writers need an initial amount of self-confidence (although many prove to be neurotic and incredibly under-confident) because it takes some nerve to believe something you want to write should be read by other people. It also takes a lot of discipline to plough your way through 100,000 words or so with only a slim chance that there will be financial reward for your effort.

On the other hand, some writers view the occupation in the way others view factory work. They turn up to the word processor, hammer away at it from 9 to 5 and leave early on Fridays. For those who are used to writing specific genres – romances, detective novels, thrillers and so on – there may not be all that much need for original creativity; you know the formula by which the story needs to be told, so you just get on and do it.

New writers will usually complete their first novel before approaching the editor of a publishing house. They need to prove that their work is good enough and that they can deliver before anyone will spend money on them. If they are fortunate they will find a literary agent who will be willing to represent them, and will take care of negotiations over how much they should be paid for the book.

If the book is successful, or if it is possible to create a 'buzz' of excitement about the publication and author, it may be possible for the agent to auction the book to the highest bidder. And again if the book proves a great success, both author and agent will be in a good position to ask for money up front for the next book. Such payments are known as advances – a fee paid before the writer has even started to work on the book.

Editor

Most editors have full-time positions within publishing companies, and depending on the publishers' activities they will usually be attached to a certain series of titles. For example, there might be a specific editor in an education publisher who handles books for the 4–7 age group, or one who handles all publications related to history.

Editors work with a number of regular authors, and it is up to them to ensure each author delivers his or her work to time and to the appropriate standard. It is the editor's job to review manuscripts when they first arrive, to make suggestions about how they could be improved, and to determine how the text should appear and be laid out within the book. The editor may also be responsible for commissioning a designer to prepare the front cover of a publication, or other artists to contribute illustrations or cartoons.

Editors are also responsible for finding new talent and bringing new authors to the publishing company. They read new submissions – or at least read those which have made it past their team of readers – and decide whether the writer has talent and can produce the kind of book the publisher needs.

Editorial assistant

This is a common first job on the editorial side of publishing. Since editors deal with many books and authors at diverse stages in the creation/printing/marketing/launch cycle, they need assistants to chase copy, check copy and generally liaise with the people responsible for other parts of the process.

Copy editor/Sub-editor

Once the editor has finalised the text with the author the manuscript will go through a process of checks and assessments prior to reaching the printing press. The copy or subeditor has the responsibility of going through the text with the proverbial fine toothcomb, seeking out misspellings, inconsistencies or typographical errors within the manuscript. It is a painstaking job and requires an incredible amount of attention to detail, but without it the publisher could be embarrassed by simple mistakes. After all, a slip of the fingers on the keyboard could replace 'from' with 'form' and no computer spell checker will flag this up.

Rights

The rights department is there to handle the legal side of book publishing. This covers everything from drawing up and managing the contract between publisher and author to managing issues such as the terms and conditions under which a book is published in another country. Conversely, if there is a book published overseas which could be good for a UK publisher to get on the bookshelves over here, the rights department will need to negotiate with the overseas publisher for this to happen.

Like other parts of the media, some areas of book publishing are driven by celebrity and gossip, so some publishers will pay celebrities a lot of money for the rights to their story or to their autobiography. They may go after people in other walks of life – from business consultants to comedians to chefs – and see if they can get exclusive rights to publish their books.

At the end of the day, publishing companies are no different from other manufacturers: they can make a lot of money by selling a unique and desired product. With the written word it is paramount that the product is protected from people who might wish to copy, use or adapt that original material without paying for it.

This can be a challenge for the written word. With book publishing it is unlikely that a publisher will make any money from reproducing the same or similar material on an internet website – the consumer must buy the book for the publisher to make any money. It is imperative therefore that the text is protected from unauthorised copying anywhere around the world. The rights department must ensure the publisher has sole right to the material being published and that no one else uses the text for financial gain. If they do, the rights department will pursue the user for infringement of copyright.

Marketing

A book may be a fantastic read but unless the public know this, and unless people can find the book in their local bookshop, it might as well not exist. Marketing roles can stretch from PR jobs such as liaising between the press and author to arrange interviews, magazine articles, personal appearances and television coverage, to liaising with bookshops and trying to strike deals whereby the shop not only stocks the book but displays it in a prominent position.

Marketing is also about striking deals with other organisations and parts of the media to secure sponsorship deals or advertising to promote the book. Marketing people need very good contacts throughout the media and book industry, enabling them to create useful partnerships and promote every publication effectively.

Like other PR roles, a marketing person in a book publisher needs to be a good copywriter for press releases, catalogue information and promotional websites. Some large publishers have a whole department dedicated to the marketing of their publications – or even to the marketing of certain titles – and there are also dedicated independent PR companies who work in this area.

Production

This is the part where the text finally hits the paper. Large publishers may have their own production departments, although they might be located away from the editorial offices. However, there are also independent printing presses that take work from a variety of publishers of diverse sizes and types. The make-up of a production company will determine the precise nature of the jobs available, but roles can include dealing with the actual task of printing – creating the printing plates themselves, working on binding a book, or sending the finished product to the client's distribution network.

Since every production house works on a number of different projects or clients at any one time, there are some very challenging administration and management roles within these companies to ensure that books are printed on schedule. At the same time, since this is where the final product is created, and so many people have invested their time and energy and talent into the creation of the book or magazine, production employees must have extremely good people skills to be able to deal with problems, last-minute requests and changes.

Brought to book

Having completed an English Literature degree course, Jane Fallows started working at a small publishing company. 'The only reason I had the opportunity was because I'd met up with the managing director of the company at a poetry reading which happened in a local bookshop,' she says. 'I didn't ask him for a job then, but I was able to show him I was interested in books, and in particular in some of the poets who he published.'

Fallows' first work within the office was, by her own admission, extremely boring. 'All I was doing was maintaining their mailing list,' she says. 'It was pretty soul-destroying stuff – just adding names onto the database, deleting multiple entries and people who no longer wanted to receive material from us.' However, since she was in the office most days she also found herself increasingly involved in other parts of the publishing company's day-to-day life. She would help organise writers' events, attend book launches and even travel to some of the international book fairs.

'In the end I found I knew a lot of people around the industry,' she explains. 'I sent my CV to a couple of companies and was offered an editorial assistant role at both of them. I was very fortunate because it meant I could actually choose which one to work for on the basis of the authors they published.'

Taking on the new job meant leaving her friends and the city where she had been studying and coming to London. At the moment, Jane is finding the financial side of life particularly challenging. 'I can just about get by on what I earn,' she says. 'But I've still got thousands of pounds of student debt and it will be at least another year before I start paying that back.' Despite this she is very happy with the work she is doing. 'It's hard work, it's challenging and I'm working on about 20 books at various stages of production,' she says. 'But this is exactly what I want to do, so I can take it!'

ALLIED PROFESSIONS

PR and communications

As noted above, not all publishing houses are big enough to have their own marketing departments. There are specialist companies that will take on responsibility for managing the launch of a book, running everything from advertising campaigns to booking public appearances and even lecture tours for the author.

Literary agent

This is the person who represents the author of the book. Literary agencies will be responsible for a number of authors and manage work across all media, so they may represent film and television writers as well as book authors. To some extent, the author's relationship with his or her agent will depend on how they came to work together. Sometimes authors receive interest from a publisher for their work, and seek out an agent to manage the contract details on their behalf. Sometimes agents read the author's work and decide it is something they would like to represent. The agent is then responsible for presenting the work to editors. Agents should aim to be ahead of mainstream literary and media trends, ready to identify new talent and able to convince publishers of this talent. They must know contractual law inside out, and always be ready to negotiate a good deal. Part of their drive towards getting the best deal hinges on the fact that they earn money by taking a percentage of the writer's fee. Therefore, the greater the amount of money the writer earns through fees, advances and royalties, the greater the agent's own income.

Media lawyer

There are lawyers who specialise in the entertainment and literary industries. They help to draw up contracts between writers and publishers, artists and producers, and so on. They may work on copyright issues and also on licensing agreements. Media lawyers might find themselves negotiating with a publisher's rights department, and need to have an awareness across the entire media industry to be able to coordinate deals that tie in television, film and print media. In the current media world, where success can be so financially rewarding and yet so fleeting, media lawyers have become an increasingly necessary part of working life. They try to ensure that those whose work has led to financial success actually get the money owed to them.

Bookseller

On the retail side of the business, booksellers are clearly an important part of the publishing industry. After all, if they do not have faith in a product or do not want to stock the book it simply will not sell. There are a number of big national and international bookshop chains which offer great careers in retail management as well as the chance to work on the front line of the book publishing industry. You should also be aware of the use of the internet for bookselling. Some sites now provide a network across the smallest of bookshops, so customers searching for rare titles have a greater chance of tracking them down.

Librarian

Libraries have been transformed substantially in recent years, and continue to redefine their role and image within the communities they serve. They used to be seen as stuffy, quiet, exclusive places – the preserve of academics, perhaps – but now they have become open and accessible. Libraries are the ideal place for members of the public to access the internet, carry out research for school, college or personal projects, rent DVDs, videos and games.

Librarians themselves have become more interactive with visitors rather than simply being the people who stamp books out and arrange them on shelves. If you want to inspire interest in books, in whatever way and to a wide range of people, librarianship is a great way of doing so.

Distribution

A logistics role and one that has similarities to distribution work for other retail industries, essentially your business will be determined by the kind of publication you are distributing.

There is obviously a difference between delivering a daily newspaper, a weekly or monthly magazine and a range of books. Distribution companies may also provide mail order services. Many booksellers now run internet sites where visitors can search for books – contemporary or rare – and order them online. Making that work requires a very good distribution service.

Magazine publishers also use mailing services to get new issues out to subscribers. Publishers outsource their mailing list function and carry out regular checks to ensure the service is getting the magazine to the right readers at the right addresses.

GETTING STARTED

Bookselling is a simple and effective way to get into the industry. Even if you just have a Saturday job manning the tills in the book section of a large retail outlet, you will be able to see how the industry works – when stock arrives, how it is promoted, how many copies are bought, how the popularity of one author or series is greater than another. It does not matter what kind of bookshop you end up working in: even a second-hand bookshop can give you useful insight, and demonstrate your willingness to work in the industry. If, however, there is a particular type of book you want to work with – art, academic, comic strip or whatever – it will be best for you to find a specialist bookshop where you can develop this particular interest while you are working.

You have to demonstrate your interest in the area of publishing if you want to be taken seriously. If you want a professional position, you should at least take a first degree, preferably in an arts or literature-related subject. Vocational study is not essential, but can help if the course offers sufficient practical experience.

Otherwise, find out as much as possible about the way the industry works, from editorial decisions through to the technical processes of printing and binding, and read all you can of the trade press. Follow developments in terms of authors, genres, outlets, use of the internet and new media for publishing and promotional uses.

The great thing about working with books is that you already know a lot of people who use these products. Everyone has a favourite author or book character. Even discussing these will help you understand what makes the industry tick – why people prefer one book to another – and why in spite of the internet, print is still an important part of everyone's life.

Get your CV out to the publishers you find interesting or who publish your favourite authors or books. And always expect your first job to be menial. As assistant to an editor, general office helper or printing assistant you may do nothing more than stuff envelopes. Don't moan about this because such tasks are still important to the smooth running of the company, and the experience gives you a good chance to watch what is going on elsewhere.

Don't feel you have to keep quiet about ideas you have for making the company or one particular book campaign more effective. Because publishers tend to be small organisations, they are ready, willing and able to take on new ideas. In some cases a small idea for a marketing initiative or to open up another readership area can have a significant impact on a company's performance and revenue with very little outlay.

3

Broadcast media: television

THE STRUCTURE OF THE INDUSTRY

Often thought of as a glamorous and lucrative profession, the world of television is not always like this, and certainly is not in the early stages of a career. Indeed, with more independent production companies now serving a growing number of satellite and cable broadcast companies, it is rapidly becoming the case that the majority of people working in television put in very long hours on programmes which are not always particularly challenging or even entertaining for most viewers. Flick through your own channel options at any time of the day or night, and spot how many 'reality' shows are being made, how many 'do it yourself' programmes, how many repeats – and how many American shows there are. The first two types of show are cheap and easy to make; the third kind is cheaper than creating a new show; and imported programming means a broadcaster can access high-quality proven shows without having to risk massive investment.

However, there is another way to look at this. Whereas writers, producers, directors and other employees in film and theatre may feel their work has greater status as an 'art' than television work, the result of their efforts will not be seen by anything like the number of people who tune into a specific channel at a specific time in order to see the latest instalment of a soap opera or the latest goings-on in a reality television show. And although some people may moan about programmes appearing to be the same, or a general 'dumbing down' of television content, there is a definite skill to creating and developing popular television formats and making them work for mass audiences.

There will always be trends within television, for both popular television and more 'arty/worthy' shows. The use of computer graphics in historic programmes, the blurring of drama and documentary for contemporary and historic recon-structions, the apparent reality television show which is actu-ally created by manipulating members of the public – all of these elements are part of the ongoing innovation of television entertainment. At the end of the day some compelling televi-sion is being made using reality techniques, while fantastic drama can be spotted in the midst of everyday soap opera.

In this fast-moving industry it is possible to make a good career from making good programmes. There are more opportunities for getting into television that ever before, and there are more opportunities of doing so outside London, as diverse production companies have found locations in the regions – from Bristol to Glasgow to Cardiff to Dublin and all points in between.

Reports from within the industry suggest this is a young people's field. Some programmes and companies positively thrive on young blood coming into their employ. This is good news for you – plenty of opportunities – but not entirely so because one sure-fire way of keeping costs down is to employ cheap, enthusiastic, talented people who have very few commitments elsewhere in their life, so can devote inordinate amounts of their time to creating television. As employees hit 30 or so, family commitments (or just the desire to have a life outside work) can significantly change the amount of time they are willing to work. Indeed, some commentators have compared television's flexible workforce with hard labour/sweatshop employment practices – where there are so many people who want to work compared with existing opportunities that the result is a workforce that can be used and dumped as required.

It is impossible to understand the television industry without starting with the BBC. Financed by the licence fee, the BBC continues to come under pressure to demonstrate that it should continue to be supported in this way and should not be an entirely private operation supported by advertising, as are the vast majority of channels. The BBC is run according to a public charter which determines what it should broadcast. The channel has to be seen to provide a public service – to make television that would not occur anywhere else – to find and deliver the best in comedy writing, drama, sport and news. It is unquestionable that throughout its existence the BBC has led the television industry, creating a number of new programme genres which have consequently been taken up and exploited by other programme makers and broadcasters.

The main competition to the BBC has always been the ITV network. Both have terrestrial channels, received through the television aerial rather than via cable or satellite. ITV has to rely on commercial revenues for its finance – the adverts which appear between and during shows – and for this reason the output has been in general more mainstream and targeted at a wider audience. In this way the station can attract more viewers and thereby offer advertisers the chance to get their product in front of a greater number of people.

Channels 4 and Five operate in the same way, although you should note how each station has clearly established its own individual identity. It is possible to identify which channel a television programme is likely to appear on because of its title, style and subject matter. This way each channel can appeal to advertisers on their own terms – if you buy advertising time with us, your ad will appear in front of more people aged 14–21 than if you broadcast on another channel, for example. Alongside advertising, channels also allow companies to sponsor certain programmes. This means details of the sponsoring company appear before and after each programme segment, theoretically linking the company with the programme for the viewer.

When it comes to cable and digital channels the same commercial rules apply. At this level, however, audience share may not be significant enough to attract the really big advertisers. For this reason, if you tune in to a less popular channel you will find the advertisements themselves are of a lower standard than those appearing on the main channels. It is cheaper to appear on a digital channel, so companies who may not be able to afford to appear on a terrestrial channel buy space here.

What does all this mean to you? It means a lot because if you are to work effectively in television you need to understand precisely the aim of the programme you are involved with, and through that the aim of the channel that is to broadcast the programme. There is no point in trying to make a wonderfully innovative and thoughtful programme about the plight of people who need to visit sunny places in order to feel rejuvenated after the pressures of home life, if all the channel wants is a cheap and easy show about the exploits of holiday reps.

BEFORE YOU START GOING ANYWHERE IN TELEVISION

- What kind of programmes would you like to make? Are you aiming for serious documentaries or do you just want to produce daily shows for daytime television? Drama or documentary, news, current affairs, history programmes – the list is endless.

- Do you want to work in live television or the recorded environment? Both offer unique challenges, and neither is the 'easier option'.

- What job do you want? Are you interested in writing shows, producing them, managing other people who make those shows, presenting shows, or just writing about them?

Mark Thompson – the new Director-General of the BBC

Interviewed when still Director of Television at the BBC, Thompson freely admitted that his career path would be near impossible to follow in today's BBC. His experience is far from irrelevant, however. Thompson's career began on a BBC production scheme and led to his working throughout the corporation in a variety of roles and positions. Always with a mind to a management job rather than programme making, he gradually progressed through managing ever larger departments and numbers of staff – from Head of Factual Programmes, to Controller of BBC2, to Director of National and Regional Broadcasting.

Thompson believes it is still possible to get this kind of career progression in the television industry, but in order to do it an individual must move around between companies and programme areas. (As if by illustration, following the interview he moved to Channel 4, before moving back to the BBC as Director-General in June 2004.)

One observation Thompson makes which does hold true is that a lot of people in senior positions in the television industry have a current affairs background. They are from factual and journalistic-type programming. 'Perhaps it's because of the 'go-getting' nature of their work,' he says. 'As a journalist you have to be inquisitive and you have to search to find your story. It's that kind of persistence and understanding that can lead your career to the top.'

(For a fuller version of this case study see *Getting a Top Job in the Arts and Media* by Simon Kent, also published by Kogan Page.)

OCCUPATIONAL AREAS

Overview

Since they are both broadcast media, television and radio share much of the same structure, and indeed both are dominated, in the public's mind at least, by the BBC. With regional studios and offices, the BBC does have a wide range of opportunities for all kinds of programme makers and employees, but this is really the tip of the iceberg. There has been a huge increase in independent television production companies – created sometimes around the strength of a single programme – and some of these companies have expanded to become international concerns, making programmes specifically for the US market as well as selling UK productions around the world.

Some of these independent companies are dedicated to creating specific programme types – Hat Trick Productions, for example, tend to be concerned with comedy – while others have become players across genres. Again, if you know what kind of programmes you want to work on, this should inform your decision about which companies you should approach for work.

Finally, as in the rest of the media industry, a large number of workers are freelance and work essentially for themselves rather than for a specific and permanent employer. This has benefits for all in the industry:

- The production companies themselves do not have to support full-time employees.

- People are employed in order to work on specific programmes. Someone with the skills to work on a documentary, for example, may not have the skills – and certainly will not have the experience – needed to work on a drama.

- Employees can move freely between programmes, gaining experience and working on what they want to work on.

▓ Teams of television professionals can get together for the creation of specific programmes, thereby feeding off each other's talents and ideas and creating ever more impressive television programmes.

The creation of a television show splits into three areas: pre-production, production and post production. There are jobs in these specific areas, and others which overreach the entire process.

Pre-production

This is concerned with the work required to set up the filming of a programme. For factual shows this requires *researchers* to explore the subject being filmed. Information needs to be found that could be included in the film. If there are experts or specific research or visuals – locations or photography – that are relevant, these too should be sourced and prepared for filming. If the programme is going out live, or features a panel or audience discussion which will appear as if live, the required people need to be found and contacted, and arrangements made to ensure they get to the studio on time. A whole host of *production assistants* will be involved in a variety of tasks to coordinate this aspect of the programme.

In fiction programmes pre-production will involve the process from the *writing* and finalising of the script through to auditioning *acting* talent and rehearsals. *Camera operators, lighting technicians* and *sound crew* will also be sourced and recruited for the period of the shoot. *Set designers, builders and decorators* will be employed to prepare external locations or studio sets depending on where the filming is to take place.

Pre-production includes much discussion about the look and feel of a programme. It will be decided what the overall effect of the programme should be – whether a documentary is essentially going to be entertaining or extremely serious in its handling of its subject, whether a drama will be a straightforward representation of events or a little more daring in its use of images and special effects. All these decisions will impact on the resources required to realise the programme, and the talent and skills and people the production needs to employ to achieve that.

Production

This is when filming actually takes place, and it is when the majority of *technical crew* are employed – *lighting and sound technicians, camera operators* and so on. This is also where *presenters* present and *actors* act. If the show is a live broadcast or 'as live', such as a news or current events programme, the director will work with technicians – *picture and sound mixers* – within the broadcast studio to mix the material as it is broadcast.

Within a studio context there will be a number of cameras covering those included in the programme from a variety of views. The director must select the right shot at the right time to create interest and present the show in the best way possible. This can mean the cueing-in of pre-recorded footage or perhaps live items from other presenters, even switching to other locations for a live link-up. In order to make this work smoothly there needs to be another set of mobile technicians and equipment working to ensure that the link – usually via satellite – with the main television studio operates smoothly and that the entire broadcast goes without a hitch.

Of course, there are all kinds of things that can go wrong with live broadcasts, and it is up to the director and his or her team to respond to emergencies as they arise and do everything they can to keep the programme on air. This possibility makes live television one of the more stressful areas of the industry, for those behind and in front of the cameras. However, once you get used to operating in this area you can feel confident and thoroughly enjoy the work.

Post-production

For pre-recorded programmes, this involves taking the material that has been created during the production phase and producing the finished programme. This means taking that material to a post-production facility, either within the television company itself or more likely run by a facilities house which has the necessary equipment for the task. While it is possible to find editing systems that run on laptops, these are not likely to be capable of producing broadcast quality programmes – they may lack the capacity to handle all the material shot, the technology to create picture effects required by the programme's director, or simply the ability to produce images with sufficient resolution (image detail).

It is now common practice to record productions on a digital video format, which is then 'digitised' into the computer edit system so it can then be cut and arranged using an editing programme. The person who carries out this task is known as the *off-line editor*. He or she works with the show's director and/or producer to realise the final show as required.

Once the off-line edit is finished, the completed show then has to go through a number of other processes before it is ready to be broadcast. An *on-line editor* will work on the programme to make sure the show conforms to technical broadcast standards. A *dubbing mixer* or *sound editor* will work on the show's audio track, mixing all the sound recorded on location, in the studio and elsewhere. There may also be a commentary track which needs recording and mixing in as narration, as well as special sound effects to coincide with action on the film.

The following two roles overreach all three stages of making a show.

The producer

The producer oversees the entire management of a programme – from establishing deadlines and ensuring every-one works to those deadlines to making sure the entire show is made for the amount of money the company has dedicated to it. Whatever the type of programme, producers need to work with a wide range of people – from both within and outside the television industry – although the precise nature of the work will be strongly influenced by the type of programme being created.

For factual programmes, the producer will work with the director in identifying contributors who should be interviewed or asked for their input. If the programme is pre-recorded they will need to draw up a timetable which determines when initial filming takes place, when and where the programme is edited and when the programme will be delivered. The producer will liaise with production executives – more senior personnel within the television company – to ensure the programme meets the standard required and ultimately fulfils the brief on which the idea of it was sold.

For fictional work – dramas, sitcoms, television films or series, soaps and so on – the producer is still responsible for getting the programme made to time and budget. However, he or she might now need to liaise with actors and their agents to ensure they are available and willing to appear in the show, and with location crew or studio managers depending on where the programme is being shot. The producer has the ultimate responsibility for the performance of everyone working on the show. If the props do not do what they are meant to do or the make-up and costume departments are not creating the right look, it is the producer's responsibility to do something about it.

The director

Directors are the people with the vision for the whole programme. They decide what exactly will be in the programme – factual or fictional – and ensure that the required material is shot. They have complete control over the process of filming itself; everyone from camera operators to the actors or presenters will answer to the director.

In some programmes the roles of producer and director are combined: sometimes because the director is also the originator of the idea, and has the necessary contacts and skills to make the programme a reality; sometimes because it is easier to create a programme like this. Since the director is responsible for the final appearance of the programme, shouldn't he or she have complete control and responsibility for making the programme happen?

With some documentaries, the director/producer might even shoot the film personally. The growth of reality/fly-on-the-wall television documentaries coupled with the ease of use of digital cameras means that a documentary can be shot by one or two people following their subject with a DV camera and some sound recording equipment. Moreover, because it is now possible to buy edit suites which fit onto a laptop computer, producer/directors can even start to edit their programmes before getting into a professional studio.

ALLIED PROFESSIONS

PR and communications

Again, there is a whole industry around PR work and communication roles since so many individuals and companies want to get on television.

Advertising

The advertising industry is also popular among those who want to work in television. With the television advert it can be possible to create a short programme or set of images which makes an impact on national and international audiences. Advertising also provides great opportunities for working across media – linking a poster campaign to a television campaign to a film cinema campaign and so on.

Advertising is a well-paid profession for those who are successful. It is an extremely competitive industry powered by young people with fresh ideas. You need to be tireless, with creative ideas, and able to explain your ideas to clients in a way they understand and appreciate.

Music video

The music industry has also created its own specialist field for using television as a promotional tool. There are some very specialist music video makers and indeed, some directors achieve notoriety for their pop promo work, no matter how short the films are and how unknown their subjects. The emphasis on using dedicated workers from the industry – certain camera people, designers and so on – means if you can get into this industry you should be able to network and continue to get work from the same team of video makers. This area of video making – together with television advertisements – is often the proving ground for innovative programme makers.

Animation

If you are a graphic artist or model maker you may want to create animated programmes – cartoons, films and advertisements. There have also been some significant full-length feature films and television programmes made using animation – the stop animation techniques of *Wallace and Gromit*, the computer generated animation of films such as *Finding Nemo*. In both cases, making animated programmes is a time-consuming and painstaking process, and you will need to undergo some kind of training before you enter the industry.

Corporate video

Businesses use video programmes for a variety of reasons. They may use them as in-house communication tools – updates and messages being created and broadcast to workers as and when required. They may need videos to explain company procedures or for training activities. Indeed, there is a very lucrative market for generic and tailor-made training videos and DVDs to help viewers develop customer-facing or technical skills.

Video conferencing and internet video conferencing technology have offered another area where television workers can get involved, from the technical side of managing the studio where the training is being held through to the scripting of presentations or pieces to camera by industry experts.

Finally, there is a small but significant domestic market for professional video makers – the creation of wedding videos or films which record significant occasions. The rise of the domestic video recorder has reduced this market substantially, but there is still a niche there for those who can sell and deliver a professional service.

GETTING STARTED

Experience is everything in television. No matter what area you want to work in, you need to get your foot in the door of a television company and work for next to nothing – if not actually nothing – to get your career on the move.

You will find all kinds of work experience opportunities across the industry, but the most common is as a 'runner', someone who runs around carrying out tasks for everyone else. This usually means making lots of cups of tea, but at least if you do this with enthusiasm and demonstrate an interest in what is going on around you, your opportunities will increase.

The BBC, both regionally and in London, runs work experience schemes, and while places on these are fiercely competed for, it is still worth an application or two. Some independent companies also run 'internships' for newcomers to the industry. Of course, there is nothing to stop you from approaching independent production companies, producers and programme makers themselves directly to ask whether you can come and work for a while, or simply watch them at work.

Facility houses are also a great source for runner positions. Since these companies basically support the work of production companies who come into their premises, you can meet a lot of different people from different companies while working there. You may find yourself taking on technical and maintenance roles – ensuring the edit machines, video players and playback screens work – or simply provide hosting services (more tea making). The point is not what you are doing now, but what you want to do, and how the information you gain from being on site will contribute to your career direction.

Wherever you find your first experience, you should be ready for a busy working life and long working hours. You may have to run around town carrying videos and paperwork from one office to another. You may need to liaise with couriers and ensure certain admin tasks are definitely carried out according to schedule. To this extent, your first job may simply feel like an office job. Again, that is no bad thing; you are after all, working in the industry.

It used to be the case that a lot of roles within the industry operated on a kind of apprenticeship model – a new editor or camera operator would learn directly from working with an established employee in this field. The increase of people trying to get into the industry, together with the decline in full-time jobs within production companies, means this structure, while not entirely absent, is no longer the norm. For this reason it is highly likely that you will need to take some kind of training, especially if you hope to become an editor or a producer. Would-be presenters and actors too will find they can pick up useful skills from dedicated courses.

You must be ready to invest in your skills – both now and in the future – and you must make sure the courses you take are respected and meaningful. In some instances attendance on a course can be enough to persuade television producers and companies that you are able to do the job. Students at the National Film and Television School, for example, can expect to leave their course and find work in their chosen profession immediately, but this is by no means an easy short cut. The courses that really pave a way into the industry are always over-subscribed and always attract the most talented and determined students. If you are to get on one of these courses you must be able to demonstrate clearly your interest, commitment and current level of ability for the business of television.

IF YOU DO NOTHING ELSE

- Watch as much television as possible, especially in the genre you wish to work in.

- Watch the end credits of every show you are interested in. Remember the names of production companies, producers, directors, writers, editors – everyone who has contributed to the show.

- Read the industry press. Know who the prime movers are in the business, see what the industry is talking about, and anticipate industry trends.

- Make your own show. If you can get your hands on the equipment, go out there and show the industry what you can do. Put together a 'showreel' which demonstrates your ability to deliver, and those in the industry will perceive you as a safer bet.

Box clever

Steven Holt works as a runner at a television post-production company in London. He finished a film studies course at university 10 months ago and hopes to end up making his own feature films. At the moment that seems a long way off.

'To be honest, I'm not sure if my work here will lead directly to me making the programmes I want to make,' he says. 'I think that's going to happen because I'm going to go out and make it happen.'

Holt's day-to-day work depends on whatever the users of the facilities require. Sometimes he just makes tea and coffee, while other days he might need to transfer 'rushes' – the initial footage from television shoots – onto the computerised edit system, a task that requires him to stay in the office until the early hours to make sure everything is recorded correctly.

'Some edits are better than others,' he concedes. 'You have some programmes where everyone knows what they're doing, what kind of programme they're making or maybe this is the second series so it's straightforward. But you also get projects which are a nightmare to work on. The equipment breaks down, the people making the programme disagree as to what it should look like – there are so many things that can go wrong.'

In the face of this stress, Holt has realised the importance of patience and teamwork. 'There's no way you can do this without listening to other people and taking on board their ideas,' he says.

It's a lesson he is now trying to apply with his own programme making. 'Even though you don't have any money you can still make things happen,' he says. 'I'm hoping to make a short film in the next few months, but the only way I can do that is to make sure everyone else gets something out of the project as well. The actors will do it for free and I'm hoping to be able to borrow some

45

equipment, but unless everyone thinks it's a good thing to work on, or that the end product will be worthwhile, there's no way it'll happen.'

4

Broadcast media: radio

THE STRUCTURE OF THE INDUSTRY

Work in the radio industry and you are working for one of the UK's most treasured media. Radio broadcasting predates television and indeed when television first started broadcasting in London it was the radio stars who made it onto the nation's screens. Radio news, plays, music and discussion programmes have played a huge part in shaping the nation – in sharing information and keeping the country in touch with itself and the rest of the world. Even today, in parts of the world radio is not a luxury – a leisure time distraction – it is an important communication resource, bringing education, knowledge, and sometimes emergency information to remote populations.

The industry currently stands on a new age. It is the advent of digital radio – the opportunity to deliver high-quality sound across the airways to diverse communities. At the same time, radio stations are being broadcast across the internet, allowing computer users to 'tune in' via a station website to access the kind of programming they want, whenever they want it. The BBC has introduced new channels, some predominantly using existing material (the BBC 7 comedy channel, for example), some broadcasting to new audiences such as the BBC Asian Network. However, this is the tip of the iceberg. There are countless other local and national commercial radio stations broadcasting to particular communities at particular times. What this means to you, as someone who wants to work in the media, is that the opportunity is there for you to get your foot in the door at some level, within organisations of diverse sizes and dealing in diverse types of broadcast entertainment.

If you are only aware of BBC Radio One on your dial then you are losing out on a range of other possibilities. While the BBC may be the national provider of radio entertainment, this is not the only place for pioneering high-quality radio. The BBC also has a network of local radio stations. These sometimes have a bad image among younger audiences, but local stations are a great place to start out and cut your teeth in the industry. They also provide a great place to try out new ideas. If you are able to create a radio show which attracts new and excited listeners within your home town, you are far more likely to be wanted by a national station later in your career.

There are also a number of commercial local radio stations. Channels such as XFM and Capital Radio broadcast to the London area. Stations such as Win FM and Viking FM (owned by Emap) broadcast to Hampshire and Yorkshire respectively. Finally, there are specialist in-house radio stations. Hospital radio, for example, provides an important service within some health organisations, keeping patients entertained when they would otherwise find lying in bed extremely depressing. In-store radio – for record shops and retail stores – has helped to enhance the shopping experience for customers. There are also dedicated university and college radio stations – excellent places for you to start and develop your career, whether you want to work on the technical side of programme making or on the presenting side.

Radio is an immediate format. It usually broadcasts live rather than recorded programmes, which means the people who work on the programmes need to be highly skilled, responsive and pretty much ready for anything. It is not simply the DJ who needs to be able to respond to a live caller on the phone, for example, but the show's producer and even the research staff must have excellent technical and people skills to deal with problems that arise. This is not just necessary for live debates or phone-in programmes –

dealing with listener correspondence, good or bad, also requires a great deal of tact.

Immediacy also means ensuring each broadcast programme appeals to the intended audience. If your programme is meant to bring the latest sounds from a particular music genre to the audience, as that show's producer or presenter you must know exactly what you are talking about. You need to know the principal musicians, their latest releases, and if possible you need to get them to talk to you on your programme first. This might be easy to do when you are working for a national station with an established reputation – you will have music promoters and artist management companies beating a path to your studio door – but if yours is a smaller station or you are just starting out, you have to be proactive.

Not only has technology altered the potential audience for radio programmes, it has revolutionised the way in which programmes are made and delivered. Just as the television industry has experienced change with the introduction of digital video and computer-based edit solutions which can fit on household computers, editing a radio programme can now be done on a laptop using digital sound recording and editing equipment. Indeed, your own home computer probably has the capacity to record digital sound, and might even have a package that allows you to add effects to that sound before playing it back.

In some stations, DJs no longer bother with operating their own CD players, and certainly the idea of a turntable using vinyl records has long gone. Nowadays most stations have their entire play list – the music to be featured on every programme – already recorded to digital format. When the DJ wants to cue in a track he or she will simply click a mouse on a computer screen and the music will begin. In some cases the DJ may be limited in what he or she can and cannot play during the programme. Some programmes and stations have a music policy which is set in stone in order to please their particular audience, and trying to offer a show that does not conform to this kind of audience simply will not be permitted. The DJ therefore might not even have a great deal of choice about the music she or he can play at any one time.

These restrictions might have more to do with the radio station's licence to broadcast than the desire of the station manager or the people who programme the airtime. Radio stations are given licences to broadcast on particular frequencies on the grounds that they offer a specific type of programme. This programming is selected for the type of audience it intends to reach, which could be a minority audience that does not currently receive programming from any other source. BBC local radio, for example, is unlikely to feature up-to-the-minute pop music, because the majority of listeners are over 25 and will not appreciate this kind of music, and listeners who want to hear it can listen to Radio One. There is no point in the local station taking listeners away from the national station.

BEFORE YOU START GOING ANYWHERE IN RADIO

- What kind of programmes do you want to make? Is there a type of music you are keen to bring to audiences, or are you more of a spoken word person?

- Do you want a front-line presentation job or a backroom production job?

- Do you ultimately want to end up working for a national radio station, or are you motivated to see your career develop in more community-specific production?

Laughing all the way to the office

Sandra Jones says she spent most of her time at university 'messing around'. Never mind the degree in economics, her real passion was performing, and over her three years she found herself working with a number of like-minded people creating sketch shows, plays and comic routines which they took to the Edinburgh Fringe Festival.

'I was a kind of Jill of all trades,' she says. 'One minute I'd be trying to write a new punch line, then performing it, then trying to convince audiences to come and see the show, then trying to work out why the lighting rig didn't work the way it did yesterday.' With this background and the contacts she had made in the comedy world – 'I wouldn't call them contacts, they're just other people doing the same thing and so you just know each other' – she was able to get on to a BBC radio production scheme. 'I always knew I didn't have the stamina or maybe the talent to make it on the stand-up circuit or through comedy writing, but I thought production was really interesting,' she says. 'There's a lot of team working involved, a lot of organisation to be done and so on, and that's still creative, but I'm not responsible for coming up with laugh lines.'

The scheme she joined consisted of working on existing radio programmes as well as having the opportunity to create and pitch her own shows to the Light Entertainment department. 'It's been a great experience,' she says. 'On some shows you really feel like you know nothing and that you're just so privileged to be able to work with these people. And we're constantly looking at and generating new ideas and trying to work out where they'd fit across the different stations and the programme schedules.'

When the scheme comes to an end Jones will have a choice of career options. She could find a permanent job within the BBC, take a job with another independent radio production company, or go freelance. 'Once you're in the right area of work and you know people you don't have to worry too much about where the work is going to come from,' she says. 'Sometimes it's nice to just go with the flow and see what turns up.'

51

OCCUPATIONAL AREAS

The size of your employer will determine the type of jobs available. The BBC, for example, employs many journalists to run its news services across radio, television and the internet. A small local commercial radio station on the other hand may well buy in an independent news service to broadcast throughout the day. In other words, it will not actually employ journalists in-house.

Some roles are very similar to those in television, and broadly speaking they can be split between technical/production roles and presenting/'on-air' roles.

Programme researcher

This can be a journalistic-type role, but may also involve answering phone calls from listeners, recording what they have to say, and in the case of phone-in shows, preparing them for broadcast on air. Researchers will find themselves called upon to do all kinds of work in all kinds of circumstances – from going to the library and looking up events from history to finding out biographical information on an interviewee who is to appear on a show, to taking a microphone and interviewing people on location or on the street. They may be sent to specific events or occasions to record what happens. In most cases it will be a question of finding material for broadcast rather than contributing material yourself.

Radio journalists

Naturally this in many ways is the same role as press and television journalism, but there are specific skills required for putting a story across in sound only rather than words or images. As an interviewer you need to ask appropriate questions so that the responses recorded can be used as 'soundbites' – succinct phrases which encapsulate the speaker's point of view. There is no point in interviewing someone and having them ramble on for half an hour if then you cannot find a quote you can broadcast.

A newsroom in a radio station will be arranged pretty much as for the print media. There will be a team of reporters working on ideas, some dedicated to particular areas of the news and overseen by an editor who decides which stories make it to the final programme. Newscasters – the people who front news programmes – often have a journalistic background, but are employed principally for their presentation skills. They will be responsible for writing their own script, and the programme editor will work with them to create the links between each report. In the final broadcast it will be down to the editor and the programme's producer to ensure the news runs smoothly from newscaster's script to pre-recorded reports to interviews with studio guests.

Producers

Just as producers in the film and television industry have overall responsibility for the creation of a film, there is a radio producer responsible for every radio programme. Again the exact make-up of this role depends on the type of programme that is being made.

If you are producing a live-to-air music show it will be your responsibility to work out the show's format and style with the presenter or DJ, to find and arrange interviews where necessary, and to create interesting features which will attract listeners and keep them tuned in. This can include phone-ins, competitions and regular features.

Some shows have excelled at what has become known as the 'zoo' format – the idea being that rather than one single presenter talking between the music, the main presenter is joined by a few other people, and their conversation and badinage keeps the listeners entertained as much as the music. The producer's role here is to make sure the conversation is interesting for listeners, does not become offensive, and is always coherent – too many people talking at once can easily become a cacophony rather than exciting radio.

Producers may also work on prerecorded shows such as radio plays, comedy shows and live broadcasts. These all require slightly different skills – the ability to direct actors in an audio play is different from moving actors around a stage. Trying to record an event such as a comedy sketch team in front of a live audience, or the performance of a live band, can also be very challenging, requiring careful attention to detail in the placement of microphones and later in the final mixing of the sound.

Production assistants

For all programmes there will be a number of production assistants who report to the show's overall producer. They may be responsible for specific aspects of the show – the cueing-in of sound effects and pre-recorded elements – and for making sure any guests brought in to take part in the show are taken care of and are relaxed and prepared. There is nothing worse than a guest on a live radio broadcast proving so nervous that his or her voice is incoherent, or worse still, he or she cannot speak at all.

Technical roles

As you might expect, keeping a radio station broadcasting effectively and audibly means using a lot of technical equipment. It is possible to find work purely in a maintenance/support role, either ensuring the broadcast equipment is in good working order and troubleshooting issues as they arise, or if there is an outside broadcast taking place, making sure the necessary equipment is on site and ready to make a successful recording.

Technical crew can find themselves working around and up against the clock in all kinds of situations and experiencing all sorts of difficulties. For this reason they often need excellent people skills as well as a level head and expert knowledge of their field. There is no point in discovering a piece of kit does not work if you cannot then discuss the implications of this with the producer and find a way around the issue.

Presenters/DJs

If you want to be the person behind the mic, talking to your adoring public, you need to be confident, knowledgeable and entirely calm in the face of any crisis. Live broadcasting is one of the most demanding and nerve-racking areas of work. Like television presenters you need to be able to think on your feet – usually while speaking about something else – and you need to be able to speak to time (if your producer tells you to fill 20 seconds before the programme goes to the news, you have to talk and not pause to ask what you should talk about). Above all you have to have a rapport with your listeners, even though there may be only you in the studio and your producer at the mixing controls.

DJs and presenters usually identify themselves with a particular audience or broadcast subject area: a type of music, an intellectual discussion programme, a phone-in, the host of a panel game and so on. It is possible to develop your career and move between areas, but if you start out as a 'zoo' format DJ on a popular music show it is highly unlikely you will end up reading the news. You also need to 'reinvent' yourself every now and then, expand the kind of work you can do and the sort of programmes your voice can appear on. This is because as time goes by tastes change, and the next generation of radio listeners will want to hear new voices talking about their music rather than some old person claiming that pop music really isn't what it used to be.

ALLIED PROFESSIONS

Since radio can use broadcasters with knowledge ranging from the best in music to the best in gardening, you can in theory find your way into a good broadcast radio career through specialising in any and every other profession. If you become a well-respected, well-informed expert on business trends, for example, you may be contacted to comment on this area whenever it is in the news. You may also be able to find yourself a niche on a regular business news programme, where your pearls of wisdom are anticipated by listeners throughout the business community.

Presentation and communication

Radio broadcasting requires a very definite talent for communicating with an audience. You may be able to use similar skills whenever the onus is on getting a message to an audience. This can include public presentations and performances – even training and teaching roles.

Technical proficiency

Radio technology is used for communications in many different circumstances. Two-way radio solutions are used by many different kinds of organisations to keep people in touch with one another when they are geographically distant. Radio operators are employed by the Army specifically to keep units in touch with their commanders. There are also communication systems in use across the emergency services, enabling the ambulance, fire and police services to respond quickly to situations when they occur. This may seem a world away from broadcast radio work, but these systems require technical experts to install and maintain them. If something goes wrong it is not just a few radio programmes or songs that go off air; it could be the difference between life and death.

DJ/music industry

DJs are critical to the music industry, in order to get artists' music heard and ultimately bought by the CD-buying public. There are many other positions in the music industry which put their occupiers among the people who influence the next trend in music or the next number one top seller.

There are DJs in the music industry other than those who work in radio. The club scene has elevated DJs to the level of pop star and record producer. It is now clear that the ability to get a party going and keep it going all night is every bit as important – indeed can be more important – than playing music on the radio.

One career

Lorna Clarke is head of mainstream programming at Radio One. She is responsible for the producers and presenters across the station's mainstream programming – from breakfast to late night. She took a radio course at a London polytechnic which included a number of work placements around the UK for a variety of radio channels, both BBC and independent. While her passion was creating music programmes, the majority of the training and work experience she underwent was based around factual programming.

Ultimately it was her passion which drove her career. She landed a job with Kiss FM – a one-time pirate radio station which successfully gained an official broadcast licence – and it was her knowledge of the London music scene that helped build the station. The station was the first to tap into the current dance and club scene, and it is interesting to note that many of Clarke's contemporaries from that time are now significant movers and shakers at Radio One and across the music industry in general.

While her rise in management has made her less 'hands-on' in the radio studio, she still views her work as ultimately creative. 'If it wasn't creative I wouldn't be doing it,' she says. 'I can be creative in terms of the people who come into the station, the people we get to work on the programmes.'

As for her success at the BBC, she says, 'It actually helps if you don't know how the BBC works because that means you have a more fearless approach to the organisation. You're not afraid of knocking on doors or telling people what you want to do. Once you're in, you can then prove your worth through the work you do.'

(For a fuller version of this case study see *Getting a Top Job in the Arts and Media* by Simon Kent, also published by Kogan Page.)

GETTING STARTED

As noted, because the industry has expanded and radio stations are now so diverse, there is no end of organisations you can write to and approach to launch your career. However, there are other things you can do to get yourself noticed and sought after:

- Start your own club night. If you don't believe there is a radio station out there that plays the kind of music you think is important, you can draw attention to it by creating your own scene. Talk a venue into giving you the opportunity, then make sure you have the equipment and music resources ready to deliver.

- Make your own demo tape. Whether you are DJ-ing at a club or messing around in your bedroom, if you think you can talk and play records, prove it. Your demo tape could be short and off the wall – a strange comic character you have come up with, who you think would work well on a specific radio programme or channel. Whatever you think would work on radio, record it and send it to every radio producer you can find.

- Find local radio stations and hammer on their doors until they let you in. This does not have to be the local BBC radio station; it could be hospital radio or even a clothes retailer's radio show. Wherever you hear something you are interested in, find out where it is made, where it is broadcast from and how to get your foot in the door.

- There are of course a whole host of courses that will train you in journalism. If radio journalism is your aim, ensure you find a course that is specifically geared to radio and offers meaningful work experience at a broadcast station, or at least within a mock -up studio on the university site.

- Create your own radio station. It might take some clever programming but you can create your own radio station online, broadcast via your website. Even if you cannot create a live broadcast – 'streaming' the audio tracks directly onto and from your site – you could still record a whole hour of playing your favourite records, talking about whatever you want to talk about, and generally entertaining your site visitors. This kind of promotion will not just increase the possibility of someone 'discovering' you, but will clearly demonstrate your commitment to this particular media.

5

Film

THE STRUCTURE OF THE INDUSTRY

The British film industry has long been regarded with admiration around the world. It is almost as if the industry is portrayed as a film hero itself – against all odds the plucky British are still capable of delivering worldwide box office hits – but the blockbusters tend to overshadow what is a very healthy industry, supporting diverse companies of every size, dealing with every aspect of film production. Some television production companies also produce celluloid entertainment, and the BBC also supports some big screen ventures. There are also a number of US-headquartered companies that offer employment in UK offices. All these companies are on the look-out for new projects – the dead cert script, the director with a new vision, the principal photographer who consistently wows the audience.

As in the television industry, work is divided up into three areas: pre-production – the creation of a script, the bringing together of the actors, director, technical support crew who will work on the film; production – when the film is actually shot; and post-production – which covers everything from editing the film to publicity campaigns which will get audiences to pay at the box office, rent the video and buy the DVD.

There are in addition a diverse range of companies that provide technical services and support to the principal production houses. They deliver their services from film to film, gaining contracts from the different production companies as and when required. The kinds of services they deliver range from lighting supplies and rigging to catering and transportation. If a company provides a service during production, it will usually need to be delivered on location wherever the film is being shot.

Companies offering post-production services – such as facility houses where editing takes place, or CGI skills (computer-generated imagery for special effects) – tend to be building-based organisations. The vast majority of these businesses in the UK are headquartered in London. That is not to say you must be based in the capital to work in the industry – there are flourishing film companies around the UK, and a very productive animation industry in Bristol, for example – but if you really want to give yourself the best opportunities, London is the place to be.

Around all of these companies and organisations exist a lot of freelance workers. Within every aspect of the business, the vast majority of film workers are self-employed, looking to work on individual films as they occur, using their skills and building their reputation to gain more work in the future. From directors and actors to camera operators, loaders (who load the cameras with film ready for shooting), make-up artists, location managers and even the producers, makers of films are rarely employed by only one company.

For this reason, a successful career in the industry depends on three factors: your proven track record, who you know, and luck. Directors very often bring together the same team of people to work on each film they direct. They certainly choose the director of photography (DOP), and the DOP in turn may have very specific people he or she wants to use as camera operators and assistants. That in turn might lead to a specific selection of lighting suppliers and riggers. This is not simply nepotism (at least not always), but reflects the fact that making a movie is a very expensive, time-consuming, complex and risky business. In order to reduce the risk, therefore, everyone wants to work with people they know, and know can deliver. This is also why some actors become huge movie stars while others languish in obscurity – it is not purely a question of talent, but of using someone who has previously impressed audiences and so will draw the crowds to see the film.

With so much money needed to make films – and all of it needs to be taken back through the box office – there are constant calls for increases in funding for this industry. The government does provide some incentives for the industry in the form of tax breaks, although recently a number of films were indefinitely postponed when the government closed what it called a 'tax loophole' which was helping production companies reduce the amount of tax they had to pay, and therefore divert more funds to film making.

In such a financially challenging industry, however, there is plenty of room for the maverick newcomer – the film maker with very little money and a lot of style – to make an impression. New technology such as digital video (DV) cameras and desk-top computer edit suites (such as Final Cut Pro and Avid) has brought the tools film makers need closer to their grasp. There might still not be anything like shooting on 35 mm film or viewing the film in a luxury Dolby-powered surround-sound cinema auditorium, but there is plenty of scope for newcomers to prove what they can do at a relatively low cost.

Of course, the main film industry is American-owned, and it is still in Hollywood where the principal companies are stationed. In order to be truly successful in this industry, no matter what area you work in, you do need to be internationally mobile – ready to work on location, whether it is the wilds of Scotland or the wilds of Borneo. Even if the UK industry only rarely produces big-budget blockbuster movies, the industry still creates talent recognised around the world as being crucial to the lifeblood of movie-going.

BEFORE YOU START TO GO ANYWHERE IN FILM

There is fierce competition for work in the film industry – at all levels. However hard you try, you may feel that there is always someone who knows more then you, who has had more experience than you, or has more luck than you – and you will probably be right on every count. Therefore:

- When entering the industry have a clear idea of what you want to do. If you want to work in lighting, say so – and do not take a job in wardrobe.

- You must know the industry. Already you should know the directors, writers and actors you enjoy. You should know the kind of movies you like and do not like. You should be ready to discuss and defend your opinions, because it is only by interacting in this way that people will take you seriously and start to trust your judgement when it comes to making movies.

- Watch every movie you can – good or bad, you will still learn from them.

- Network like crazy. Hang out where film people hang out; read magazines, books, articles about the film industry. Know what is going on when, where and with whom.

Screen dream

'There's nothing to compare with the excitement and teamwork you get on location,' says James Kenworthy. 'Even when you're really tired and worn out you don't care – there's always something interesting going on.'

Kenworthy has been in the movies for 18 months. With a few GCSEs to his name and a fanatical interest in film, he decided to see whether he could get into the movies without any more study. After a few months of sending out CVs and phoning up employers he was offered the chance to work as a runner on a feature film being shot in the UK. 'It really was one of those chance things,' he says. 'I'd been phoning up every film company I could find in the book – well, several books actually – and just kept asking if there were any opportunities going.'

The lucky break came when one of the people Kenworthy rang said a film was looking for extras – people who would turn up and stand around for the crowd scenes. 'I turned up for an audition and they took my details, and I asked about the chances of working behind the camera. At the time they said they didn't think it would work out, but a few weeks later I got a call from a production assistant and that was it.'

Working for no money, James admits he did an awful lot of 'running' for the film – everything from helping with the lighting rig to cleaning the site when everyone else had left. 'There was nothing I didn't do, nothing I wouldn't do,' he says. 'I think the reason they liked me was that in the end I was so on the ball I actually started to predict things they would need before they realised they needed them.'

With this role in the bag, Kenworthy not only has a great deal of experience in the production of a film, he has a lot of contacts with people who work directly in the film industry. 'Two or three people have already phoned me about some projects they're setting up,' he says. 'And I know I can use their names to get my foot in the door with other companies as well. I don't mind what I do at the moment – although I'm keen to get into camera work, but right now I'm happy just to be working in the industry. And who knows, next time I might even get paid!'

OCCUPATIONAL AREAS

Scriptwriters

The people who create the blueprint of the movie, scriptwriters are often considered to be at the end of the food chain when it comes to the film industry. Sure, they may write the dialogue, describe the setting for the action, plot incredible and compelling stories, make audiences laugh, cry and scream, but their work will only reach the screen via the vision of the director. Also, the final film can be influenced by many other people and factors in the process – from the amount of budget available for the special effects to the fact that a producer thinks there should be a happy ending rather than a sad one.

Screenwriters have to be driven – they could be considered born rather than made – because so much of the work is done alone at a word processor, only to be ripped apart by a film producer or director who sees things differently. Scriptwriters must be able to take these kinds of blows on a regular basis, to know when to accept and work with the ideas of those around them, and when to dig in their heels for the good of their movie script.

Location managers

Depending on the size of the production, being a location manager may simply mean working in the pre-production phase and finding suitable places where the film can be shot, or it may mean doing this and then managing the location itself during shooting. The finding of locations can be an exhausting and difficult process. Not only do you need to find somewhere the director likes the look of, you need to negotiate with the owner to get his or her permission to use the location.

You then need to make sure the site is ready for everyone else when they turn up to shoot the film. Is there enough space for all the lorries, trailers, cars and so on? During shooting nothing untoward can happen around the location to disrupt the process. The location manager must therefore make sure no members of the public walk into shot, and no noise other than that required for the film is heard.

At the end of the day's shoot the location manager has to make sure the location is returned to its former state – clean up any mess, repair any damage and make sure the owner is happy.

Producers

Producers have overall responsibility for the creation of the movie. This is a coordinating role, liaising with other senior people connected with the movie, making sure the wardrobe, design and even the catering services deliver what they are meant to deliver on time and to an appropriate standard. The producer works on a film project from the very beginning to the very end of the process. Producers help out on finalising the script, sometimes help find the finance to make the film, and are still there when the final edit is made and the movie has its premiere. In spite of all the administration involved, producers are still very creative people. They have an immense impact on the movies they work on – it is they who bring together the team who will deliver the final product, and getting this right will create a unique and successful film.

Directors

The director has ascended to such importance in the film industry that films are now credited as being 'by' the director, rather than the writer or anyone else. The director has the responsibility for taking the scriptwriter's blueprint and turning it into a reality. He or she must determine the look and feel of each scene and ensure every scene is shot correctly. The director has control over everything, from the look and feel of the set and lighting to the performances of the actors.

Directors sometimes have their own particular identifying styles – there may be certain visual aspects of a film that make it theirs, or alternatively they may be associated with specific genres such as ghost stories, action adventures or period romances. In general directors receive scripts for consideration from scriptwriters (or more likely from scriptwriters' agents), and if they are attracted to a project they will sign up to the film at that point. Others work regularly with certain producers, so scripts may be passed their way by the producer. They may also be approached by production companies who have already secured funding for a project and are looking for a good director to take it on board. Finally, writer-directors create their own film scripts and are therefore responsible for the entire creation of the film.

While the director's priority is always to realise the full potential of the film using the resources available, the director must also try to complete the film on time and to budget. While it often falls to the producer to ensure that these targets are met, a director will soon gain a negative reputation if he or she is forever costing the production company more money than was initially budgeted.

Camera operators

Every film has a director of photography who determines the best way to achieve the shot required by the director. The camerawork itself requires the teamwork of many people in order to ensure the material required is captured. For example:

- The *focus puller* ensures the camera lens is always adjusted so that the picture is in focus.

- There may be a number of people known as *grips*, whose job it is to move the camera to follow the action.

- In some cases the camera may be mounted on a trolley on a small track so it can follow the action smoothly. *Track layers* handle this aspect.

- The *clapper loader* is responsible for ensuring the film cartridge is loaded properly before shooting and that film once shot is cared for correctly.

Editor

The editor is the person who takes the material shot for the film (known as rushes) and cuts the scenes together in order to create the film. The editor works closely with the director during this process, since there will be scenes, images and incidents that the director wants to include to create his or her vision of the film. At the same time, the editor brings his or her own influence to the film, identifying the best ways to tell the story and to bring the characters and performances to the screen. It is a time-consuming process – there are plenty of rushes to view and all kinds of different ways a scene can be edited to give it the best look and the best rhythm within the film as a whole.

In the last 10–15 years technology has revolutionised the role of the editor. There was a time when every film – for either television or the silver screen – was shot and edited on actual film. This required the physical cutting and sticking-together of film according to the frame where each scene started and ended. Nowadays companies can shoot their productions on digital tape, edit digitally, add in or change images using computer graphics, and only then transfer the finished product to a 35 mm film print.

Sound recording and mixing

Sound is of paramount importance to the success of any film. Sound opens many possibilities for the film maker in terms of establishing mood, creating atmosphere, tension or humour. On low-budget films where resources are tight, it is always a good idea to make sure the sound recording is the best it can be. It is easier to use a shot if it is out of focus but has good sound than it is to use an in-focus shot that has poor-quality sound.

On location, sound recordists capture dialogue and back-ground noise. There may be a team of people working on this, using a combination of sound-recording equipment – boom microphones, radio microphones and receivers. In the studio the same care is required to get a good sound track, although obviously the sound recordist here does not have to worry so much about background interference (aeroplanes heard over-head midway through a period drama scene, for example).

In the area of post-production there are roles such as sound designer and mixer – people who work on creating the final soundtrack for the film. Workers known as Foley artists record extra sound effects to coincide with on-screen action. For example, if there is a scene in which someone walks across a gravel path, it may be easier for the sound of the footsteps on gravel to be added after filming has taken place.

The final sound mix of a film is an extremely complicated task because there are so many different sources from which sound can come. This is not simply a matter of ensuring all the sound recorded on location and in studio is usable and audible. The sound track will often include music, either orchestral or pop songs, which might be specially written and recorded for the purpose.

Publicity and promotion

Even before a film is made, the film studio must invest time and resources to ensure audiences will go and see it. An effective campaign means arranging for the film actors to do interviews and public appearances, and organising high-profile coverage at the film's first showing – which might involve a massive red carpet in Leicester Square in London, or a first glimpse at an international film festival. Campaigns are now launched across all media – television spots, SMS updates, promotional incentives with other products (special offers on the back of cereal packets and so on) and websites carrying trailers, interviews and images. All these activities have jobs associated with them.

ALLIED PROFESSIONS

Given the wide variety of roles required for making a film, it is actually possible to work in any profession at all and be a part of the movie industry.

Films need accountants, for example, to make sure all their financial requirements are taken care of, that the correct tax is paid to the right governments, and that the final box-office income does actually make the film a financial success. At the same time, a chef could become part of the catering team on location for the film industry, or if you like driving cars or fancy being a taxi driver, why not become a driver on location for a film – transporting actors, materials and equipment from place to place?

The movies themselves support a whole host of other industries. The studios producing big blockbuster movies will strike merchandising deals with manufacturers of toys and games, clothing and household goods. Merchandising rights operatives work on getting film characters plastered over lunchboxes, coffee mugs and baseball caps. Video game producers will want to snap up the rights to converting action adventure films into interactive shoot 'em up adventure games.

The film industry supports cinema staff, video and DVD sales outlets and hiring companies. Even if a film does not clean up at the box office, there is always the chance that it will do well on video release and who knows, if it is repackaged with lots of extra footage on DVD people might buy more than one copy. It may seem far-fetched to say you work in the film industry if you are just taking tickets at your local multiplex cinema, but these entertainment locations require good management talent to ensure all the films they show attract a good audience and leave the audience satisfied.

GETTING STARTED

There is no way you will get anywhere in this industry without proving your interest, commitment and determination for the making of films. Whether you go into the industry through work experience or after completing higher or further education, no one will give you the time of day if he or she gains the impression that you are just doing it because it seemed to be a good idea. The industry is driven by passion, and you need it from day one.

Second, even if you take a vocational or higher educational qualification, the first job you will get anywhere in the industry will be basic and low-paid – if paid at all. You will probably start as a runner, the term given to general dogsbodies who work throughout the industry and simply 'run' about for other people.

Within post-production and office-based companies runners are still used – and pretty much for the same tea-making/message-carrying duties. The important thing here is that you learn exactly how a film is made by observing and helping everyone around you, and you impress everyone with your excellent service, enthusiasm and unwavering commitment. Who cares if it's midnight or three in the morning and you have not slept for two days? You must still be ready and willing to take the post to the postbox down the road and put the kettle on when you get back. Indeed, if you make good tea you will get the best start your career can have.

If you do take a vocational qualification you may find you can get into the industry at a higher level. People who attend film school, for example, will in general be able to enter the industry doing what they have trained to do. However, they will only be able to do this because they have used their time at film school to get the right experience. They will probably create a 'showreel' – clips from films and programmes they have worked on, designed to impress employers. And because competition for getting into film school is so high, those who manage to get a place there must already have demonstrated unquestionable talent and commitment – another indication therefore of a good film worker.

It is sometimes possible to launch a career without waiting for the rest of the industry to provide you with your lucky break. Because the cost of DV cameras and editing equipment has fallen so dramatically, it is possible to make a low-budget original film that could make a huge impact on the industry. Moreover, the internet is fast becoming the place to show your film and thereby launch your career. With the ever-increasing speed of broadband connection, there are now dedicated websites where film directors can load up their short films ready for the viewing public to watch and appreciate.

While creating such films requires special consideration – after all, it is likely that most people's internet connection will only support a very small video image – it does mean anyone can get their film produced and shown around the world without having to make too large a financial outlay.

6

New media

THE STRUCTURE OF THE INDUSTRY

In the early to mid-1990s the internet became the undisputed new frontier for business. The popularity of home computers created a brand new route through which companies could reach their customers. Not only did every existing company need a website, but the internet spawned countless new enterprises, some consisting of only one or two people. All of those involved believed they would soon be millionaires through offering website design and management services. The internet was not just a marketing tool or new shop front; it was a way to bring together companies from around the world, to connect different parts of those companies, enabling them to do business together in an efficient and unprecedented way.

At the same time the traditional media – newspapers and broadcasters – recognised both a threat and an opportunity through the internet. With an easy-to-use web browser anyone could access news, current events and information about everything he or she wanted, without having to go out and buy a newspaper or watch a television programme. Viewers or readers would be able to determine what they read and what was in front of them. Clearly all traditional media outlets had to get online as fast as possible. However, they also needed to find a way of generating revenue out of this online presence – there was no point in just putting online what would otherwise appear in print, if it meant customers simply received the information they wanted for free.

And so the 'dot com boom' occurred. This was shortly followed by the 'dot com bust' when many of the small dot.com companies found out that there was not enough money around to support every new business. Some of the revolutionary new internet companies discovered that what at first appeared to be a great e-business opportunity actually attracted no e-customers and was therefore a complete waste of time.

Today, the industry is more mature. There is a steady flow of demand from customers, matched by a steady flow of new investment in start-up companies. There is less hype around, customers generally know what the internet can do and what they want it to do for them, and as a result it is a challenging and rewarding environment to work in. Organisations do not simply want a flashy website for the sake of it, they have to see the site generate real business and deliver definite returns. Traditional media organisations have become savvy to the technology. They now provide certain services – interactive and archive features, for example – which are impossible to deliver across the printed page. And what is more, they can get site visitors to pay for the privilege of accessing certain areas, or sell advertising space and links in the same way that they sold advertising space on the printed page. At the very least their websites glean useful information about their readership, allowing them to tailor the service for these people and demonstrate to their advertisers exactly who is visiting the site and for what purpose.

The watchword for the future of the industry is 'convergence'. This relates to the way in which the various forms of communication technology – television, radio, computer, even landline and mobile phone – are being used in conjunction with each other to get the maximum involvement and interaction with the audience. Already there have been television programmes where statistics and surveys have been carried out using the viewer's cable or satellite remote control keypad. Television and radio programmes now have their own websites, created by the programme makers and broadcasters to provide more information or just added entertainment relating to that programme. As with *Big Brother*, in the future the entire outcome of drama programmes may be influenced by the number of people who vote in a particular way via their mobile phones or computers.

Publicity and promotional campaigns are now designed to run across diverse media. Web programmers are not simply charged with creating a 'stand-alone' website, but elements from that site – perhaps the style or interactivity – must also be used across mobile phones through the use of text messaging. The same style should be reflected in campaigns within the print and broadcast media. To be effective in this area therefore does not simply mean mastering a computer language or two; it requires a clear understanding of how these technologies can be used to work together effectively and coherently.

Today, the industry that exists is described by insiders as 'a real meritocracy'. In other words, the only thing that will get you a good job and a successful career will be the high standard of your own work. This also means that you will only ever be as good as your last piece of work. If it is certain you can deliver what the client wants, to the timetable and budget, you will be very popular. If it becomes known that you are not able to deliver on time, this will also become known and have an adverse effect on your career.

BEFORE YOU GO ANYWHERE IN NEW MEDIA

- Make sure you are enthusiastic and completely driven in this area. The pace of technological change is relentless, which means you are unlikely to ever be able to rest at a certain skill level and take it easy.

- Be ready to work with anyone and everyone. There is no point in being a technical wizard if you cannot communicate that wizardry to other people. To be successful you must be able to understand your clients' wishes in relation to their website design and function, and you need to be able to explain what you can and cannot do, and why you can or cannot do it.

- Success will be determined by your own hard work and dedication – and that means long hours and constantly learning new skills.

No rest for the on-IDLE

Ané-Mari and Marc Peter are Managing Director and Creative Director of on-IDLE, a web design and development agency. Both agree working in the industry is not a nine to five occupation. They are engaged in networking activities (with possible clients and working partners) at least three evenings a week, and regularly pull late hours, whether working on a client's site or researching the latest technology used in the industry. 'Every month there's an update of some kind of software,' says Marc Peter. 'Or alternatively there will be an entirely new technology you need to understand.'

Marc Peter studied typography at college, gaining a traditional design-led professional qualification. While this has meant further study for him to get to grips with web technology, he feels it has given him a very good grounding in the discipline of design, which some multimedia courses can neglect. 'There is a danger that students know a lot about coding and programming but nothing about how design, fonts and colours work,' he says.

Now that they have created their own private limited company, Ané-Mari recommends that high-flying and ambitious young people who want to succeed in the business take a similar approach. 'As long as you find someone with the business knowledge to manage that side of your operation you can work towards your own goals,' she says. 'A private limited company means that even if things go wrong you are not likely to lose your own personal money.'

That said, the idea of course is to grow your company, gain more orders from clients and to be thought of as one of the best agencies in the country – and that also depends on your networking skills and market profile. The Peters believe the UK, and London in particular, provides a great arena for this kind of work to take place. Whereas some European companies and practitioners can be tight-lipped and protectionist about their work, the UK's website developers are keen to share ideas – about both the technical creation of site functionality and the nature of contracts and agreements drawn up between the web developers and their clients. 'It's a much more demanding market than it used to be,' says Ané-Mari. 'But it's also more realistic. The daily rates for programmers are no longer hundreds of pounds – but the whole industry is a little more secure than it was.'

OCCUPATIONAL AREAS

With such a diverse range of organisations operating in new media, you will find job roles and functions vary between companies according to the size of organisation and the type of work it is engaged in. In general, however, all roles split into creative or technical disciplines.

Content writers and editors

Like their print media counterparts, these roles are concerned with the gathering and presentation of information for website visitors. New sites still require journalists to create copy, editors to determine content and sub-editors to ensure the copy is suitable for the website. Naturally with smaller organisations all of this work may be done by one person.

Within some new media agencies, writers may be used to create copy specifically for client websites. In other words, they have more of a corporate nature to them rather than news or features. The work may entail collecting information from around the organisation, or learning about a particular product or service which then needs to be presented on the website. If a website is designed to be interactive with its visitors, it may fall to the editor to receive contributions from visitors and edit these before presenting them on it.

Designers and programmers

These employees decide the best way to present information across the website, and work on the programme code that is used to make this happen. These roles require people who are not only enthusiastic about design, but keen to continually update their skills and keep track of the technology being used in new media to create new effects and interactivity. Indeed, half the job can entail reading and learning new skills as the technology progresses.

The exact position and type of job is likely to be dictated by the programming skills the individual has. Different companies look for C++ programmers, people who can handle Java and/or people who know all about the latest Macromedia tools.

It is crucial to ensure that a website can be viewed satisfactorily by any computer interface which can access the internet. This means not only do successful workers need to be up to date with website programming techniques, they must be aware of and ready to adapt to changes in the wider technology used. If Microsoft or Apple introduces a new system, or changes to its existing systems, every programmer needs to be ready to make his or her code work on that platform.

This is no place for the 'techie' who hides away behind a computer keyboard. It may well be that you do not work directly with clients, but you will need to work with the other people within the organisation. Very often solving a website problem or challenge means sharing programming ideas and helping each other out. No one will want to work with you if you keep all your ideas to yourself and will not listen to the ideas of others.

Account managers

A role recognisable from the advertising profession, account managers are the people who talk to a media agency's clients, identify campaigns, initiatives and events they wish to commit to, and make sure these projects are completed satisfactorily. One of the hardest aspects of the job with new media is dealing with the continual change in technology. It is possible to decide on the creation of a website only to find the technology has moved on so much that by the time the site is due to go online it is possible to do much, much more on it than was originally thought. Account managers must also be able to reassure and placate their clients in the event of the – almost inevitable – breakdown of technology: the website that cannot cope with the number of visitors it attracts, the 'hijacking' of a website by malicious hackers, and so on.

ALLIED PROFESSIONS

Technical programming

If you are a wizard at computer programming, particularly for communications purposes, you can find all kinds of work developing and maintaining computer systems within industry. Organisations need to be able to access and share information swiftly and efficiently and with the minimum number of computer problems. Very often organisations have legacy systems – old computer systems which retain details of past customers, sales and business. Rather than do away with this information completely, some computer consultancies provide solutions which give access to these old systems, enabling them still to be used in a valuable way.

Computer systems are being used across businesses in new and innovative ways. They are being used to track, record and manage employee information, to arrange shift work and record employee activity. Even if these systems provide technical support to an organisation, they still need to be easy for the end user to understand and operate.

Communications and PR

Rather than doing the work yourself, you can be a consultant in the field of IT, identifying the best way companies can use the new media at their disposal, and liaising between the client and programmer to make sure a suitable solution is developed and implemented.

Games industry

This is a vast industry which is attracting enormous investment for new ideas and development. Such is the market for computer games now that some games attract funding comparable to big-budget feature films. The industry thrives on creative ideas and technical talents to realise the games. Multi-level adventure games now compete on delivering complicated and challenging game plots where users have near-complete choice in what they do within the virtual games world. Technical programmers are employed in teams to work on specific aspects of a game – everything from sound design to texture of surfaces to ensuring players cannot walk through walls. It is a fiercely competitive industry and hard to get into, but with everyone looking out for the next big trend in games, if you have what it takes you can develop a lucrative and highly successful career.

Broadband business

Now the industry has calmed down a little there is great activity occurring within service suppliers as they try to get the UK to take up broadband internet solutions and combine these with ever-cheaper phone and cable/satellite television options. If you are looking for a sales, management or even technical role, but do not have a truckload of programming qualifications, these companies could be your starting point in the industry.

Marketing your own value

Kat McClure is Marketing Manager at Minstrel Internet, but her career has led her through Polygram Records, Disney and many other media organisations. 'My career really took off because I starting temping,' she says. 'Even if you're just answering phones or doing basic admin work, temping is a great way to get your foot in the door of the industry.'

McClure was halfway through a business and German degree when she was offered a position at Polygram Records. She had already worked for the company through a temping agency, and she knew this was the industry and role she wanted to take. 'Although I left my degree course and took the job I didn't stop studying,' she says. 'I was working a full week and then studied two evenings a week – six hours in total – for my advanced certificate in marketing and for a diploma in marketing. That meant I had a professional degree as well as industry experience.'

Having moved from the music industry to television and now to an internet service provider (where, as a bonus, salaries are significantly higher), she has found she can apply the same marketing skills to each area while gaining new knowledge on how each industry works.

Moreover, McClure now recruits people into the industry herself, and one of her top tips is to ensure you include a fantastic covering letter with every CV you send out. 'A good covering letter tells me more about the person who's applying than the CV,' she says. 'If you're 16 to 18 years old, the chances are you will not have had much of a chance to work in the industry, so your CV may not be that long. The covering letter is therefore the place to show how much you want to work in the industry and how passionate you are about the work.'

Her second piece of advice is to make the most of any and every kind of relevant work experience you have. If you have helped promote a band, made a video or created an internet idea, make sure your potential employer knows about it. Even if you have just worked in an office this can still be relevant work experience, regardless of whether the office was part of the media industry. 'Don't be afraid of ringing people up and asking them for work experience or career advice,' says McClure. 'Sometimes you'll get a piece of advice that makes all the difference – and at least it means employers are aware of you.'

GETTING STARTED

You will not get anywhere at all unless you have experience. The fact is that there is so much competition for work out there that there is very little reason for anyone to get a job on the basis of 'Let's give them a go and see what happens.' If you are just starting out on your career, obviously you will not have had a great deal of opportunity to get experience, so here are a few ways of doing it:

- Take a sandwich course. If you go into further education for three or four years, take a course that includes lots of opportunity to work in the industry. You need to apply the theoretical or practical skills you use in the computer lab to the real world outside.

- Go into the industry, start work there, and take a vocational course as soon as possible. You might start with a relatively low-paid, low-responsibility job, but you will have experience of working in the real workplace. If you need technical or professional skills you can pick them up and apply them immediately. And you might even be able to get your employer to pay for your course, thereby avoiding student debt.

- Do it yourself. If you want to work in new media you should already be capable of delivering web pages, basic IT programming and so on. You should know what the best programs are, the best web page designers and the future of interactivity on the web. You should definitely have your own home page, and if at all possible you should have extra links on that page which take visitors to yet more samples of your work. Imagine the impression you will make in an interview if you can simply ask your interviewer to log on to a specific website to see what you can really do.

- Set up your own company. It may be tough out there but it is by no means impossible to set up your own company and start from scratch. You may need to find a business guru/expert to guide your strategic direction and help you out with the legal side of things, but if you believe you can do well in this industry and do not feel you need to be shaped, developed, held back or restricted by an existing organisation, there is nothing to stop you from going it alone. With limited company status you can protect yourself from financial liability if everything does go wrong – although obviously this is not an excuse for blowing it because you cannot be bothered to put in the work required. It is very hard work to go it alone, but if you are successful the rewards can be immense.

- Network and make friends. Even employees a few years into their career still devote a significant amount of their time to keeping up with what is happening with the industry. They meet friends, colleagues and even competitors in official and unofficial ways. The technology moves so fast that there really is not that much of a 'competitive edge' that can be achieved by one person's programming skills. Sooner or later everyone else is going to know how to do it, or find an even better way to do the same thing. Far better, then, to share problems, triumphs, gossip and everything else besides.

■ Your networking will keep people aware of your work, and keep you aware of what is going on across the industry. If there is a project you would particularly like to get involved in, this is the only way you will find out. The vast majority of opportunities will not even be talked about, let alone presented in the trade or national press. If two people discuss a new project they will probably have identified suitable people to do the work before they have finished deciding what precisely the work will entail.

■ It doesn't matter how tenuous your link to the industry might be. Exploit it for all it is worth. Even if it is simply that your next-door neighbour's mum's cousin is related to someone who knew someone who worked with someone in the same building as the company you would like to work for, believe it or not that is a way in.

■ Don't underestimate the experience you have had. It does not matter if you have just surfed the web and compiled a list of useful websites for the school magazine – that is relevant experience. If you have worked in an office – any office – that is relevant experience. If you play a lot of computer games, that is also relevant experience within the industry. Indeed, it may be you can get your first job in the industry as a games tester. Just approach the games with a critical eye – find out who wrote them, made them, programmed them, and consider how you might be able to make something similar – or better.

WHEN APPROACHING EMPLOYERS

■ Make sure you know exactly what it is they do and how you will fit into their employment structure and working culture.

■ Always write a covering letter with every CV. This letter can be more important than the CV, because in it you will demonstrate beyond the shadow of a doubt your enthusiasm, commitment and determination to succeed.

- Make sure you have a portfolio with examples of relevant work. Again, if you want to work in the design of websites but do not yet have the technical skills or resources to make your own, create some clear visual presentations of possible websites. Show that you are thinking about this and want to learn how to do it. An employer is not at all interested in a bunch of excuses why you have done nothing as yet.

7

Top tips

Network, network and network again

If there's an event which you're interested in, go to it. If there's the chance to talk to someone in the company you want to work for, talk to them. If you have half a chance for half a minute's chat with anyone remotely connected to the industry, take that chance. If lots of people keep asking you what you want to do for a living, don't just tell them, follow it up by asking them what experience or contact they have had with the industry, and see if there is something you can use or exploit.

It doesn't matter what you do first, just make sure it is in the industry

Work in the snack bar in a television or broadcasting company. Work in an office of a media organisation. Work as a film lab assistant.

Be prepared to move around a lot geographically

Do this not just because there might be the ideal opportunity for you in Edinburgh rather than Bristol, but because the Bristol company you work for might need you to travel to Australia to work on a project.

Find out how things work

If you are heading for publishing, get to know the physical process of making a book. If you are researching for a television show, find out the process behind production. The more you understand how a company, industry and individual project works, the more employable you become.

Send out your CV, and keep sending it

If you are trying to get work experience or a first job by sending out your CV on spec to a number of different companies, send it every three months or so. There are two reasons for this. First, you can update your CV each time, and second, companies receive so many CVs that you need to ensure yours is always towards the top of the pile. Also phone up the company you are sending it to each time, and ask whether they want it on paper or as an email attachment. Oh, and while you are on the phone, ask whether there are any jobs going.

8

Self-assessment tests and questionnaires

It is extremely rare for any media organisation to use assessment tests or questionnaires in order to assess whether an individual applicant is suitable for a first job within the industry. If you end up taking a leadership or management role you might be subjected to aptitude or skill tests or even psychometric profiling, but this will be to determine your management potential and style rather than whether you are a good media worker. Even then, within large employers promotion occurs through the results and achievements you have to your name, rather than whether you can pass an assessment test.

What is more likely, certainly if you intend to be on the creative side of the industry – working in journalism, as a copy editor or proof reader, or whatever – is that you will face tests that assess your technical understanding of the English language, your attention to detail and your general knowledge about the subject area you would be covering in your daily work.

ENGLISH AS SHE IS WRITTEN

The last thing that book publishers, newspapers, magazines and online publishers want is for there to be significant errors in the use of English. While some publications are able to take liberties with the language – indeed, for some writers it is important that they use the language in a specific way to identify readers and communicate with them – other publications will find themselves under siege from readers who can spot a split infinitive or misplaced apostrophe a mile off.

Try the following tests.

Common spelling mistakes

Identify and correct any incorrect spellings in the list below:

1. accomodation

2. the affect

3. fulfill

4. indispensable

5. abysmaly

6. personel

7. guarenteed

8. necessarily

9. targetted

10. the stationery car.

(Answers are on page 94.)

Use of English

Which of the following sentences is correctly punctuated?
1.

    A   For the sales conference, Alison has to check the seating, the lighting, the pen situation and the catering.

    B   For the sales conference, Alison has to check the seating, the lighting, the pen situation, and the catering.

    C   Neither sentence.

2.

    A   Although he could not be sure of his map reading, he decided to turn left at the next junction.

    B   Although he could not be sure of his map reading he decided to turn left at the next junction.

    C   Neither sentence.

3.

    A   Yes – he interjected, for he had to say exactly what he felt.

    B   Yes; he interjected, for he had to say exactly what he felt.

    C   Neither sentence.

Identify the incorrect sentence:

4.

    A   From the age of three it was clear that Alison was going to quickly go to the top of the class.

    B   From the age of three it was clear that Alison was going to go quickly to the top of the class.

    C   Neither of these.

5.

    A   Wishing the department to succeed, new staff were taken on.

    B   It was clear that the Prime Minister has written off the by-election result; he intended to blame it on the recession.

    C   Neither of these.

6.

    A   After having finished the exam, the candidates felt a great sense of relief.

    B   Feeling tired of the run, Hope decided to take a bath.

    C   My mother accused me of being mad, talking to myself all the time.

    D   None of these.

Make your choice: in some of the following sentences one of the underlined words or phrases is incorrect in terms of English usage. None has more than one error. If you find the error, choose the appropriate letter. If there is no error choose the letter D.

7.   A   B

Of the two dogs *that* the family *owns*, the Labrador is the

   C   D

fatter. No error.

8.   A   B

If you *were* to put *fewer* than five items in the shopping

               C   D

basket, you *could* go through the express checkout. *No error.*

9. A   B

Taking vitamins is a way of *insuring* long life, according to the

   C   D

current thinking. *No error.*

10.   A

Morphine and other p*otentially* addictive drugs are valuable

                          B

medically; if abused, however, *it* can cause untold damage.

   C

No error.

(Again, answers are on page 94.)

REASONABLE LOGIC

Another form of test assesses a candidate's reasoning and logic skills. You may be given a passage of text to read followed by a series of statements. You must decide whether the statements are true or false. There are four possible answers to each question: both statements are true, both are false, A is true but B is false, and A is false but B is true. Try the following:

Mrs Brewer, the office manager, was charged with responsibility for replacing the existing photocopier. The specifications were to remain the same in that the machine was to be able to make 50,000 copies a month, operate at least at 40 copies a minute, have the facility for double-sided copying, a feed tray and a sorter bin. She was told that she could consider ex-demonstration or new machines but must not purchase a service agreement.

Mrs Brewer embarked on the task with some apprehension as she was well aware of the bad reputation of photocopier sales staff. She decided to write out a list of specifications and sent this to a number of companies requesting written quotations and details of their products. Soon afterwards, she started to receive calls from the company representatives offering her all kinds of deals.

Questions

1.

A: Mrs Brewer requested that the sales representatives telephone her.

B: She wanted a machine which could handle double-sided copying.

2.

A: A service agreement was to be part of the deal.

B: More features were required of the new machine.

3.

A: Mrs Brewer requires the sales representatives to send her two types of information.

B: She has a preference for a new machine rather than one which has been reconditioned.

4.

A: While she was apprehensive, Mrs Brewer was able to take some consolation from the fact that she was not solely responsible for the decision over which copier to purchase.

B: Photocopier sales staff have a reputation.

YET MORE LOGIC

Each question makes a statement relating to a passage. You need to say whether the statement is true, false, or it is impossible to say. Answers must be based on the information in the passage ONLY and this information is to be accepted as true. The passage:

> Peter shared a father with Hilary but it is not Steven, the father of John, youngest son of Silvia (who is Hilary's mother).

Questions

Answer True, False or Not possible to say.

1. Silvia had three children.

2. Steven is the father of at least two of Silvia's children.

3. Silvia is Peter's mother.

4. John is the offspring of Steven and Silvia.

Same test but the other way around

Rather than give you the task of identifying the correct answer, some employers may give you a straightforward journalistic or editorial task to complete. They give you a passage of text relevant to your area and require you to edit/sub-edit and correct the piece – identifying errors in the spelling of company and organisation names, technical information and so on. Alternatively, they may give you the raw material – press release and interview copy – for a news feature and give you a set time in which to produce an article to a certain number of words. Such tests might exclude the use of word processors and certainly do let allow you to use spellcheckers.

LOGICAL PRACTICE

Clearly the only way to prepare for such tests is to practise. Set yourself a wide range of projects to complete, from creating

800-word news stories on events around the area you live to rewriting important national news stories, demonstrating your understanding of a situation, to producing your own 'column' – a piece about what you have been doing recently and what you see around you.

Any kind of reporting, writing, or creation of written, spoken or recorded material will help you sharpen your skills, find your style and build your portfolio.

All the test material in this chapter is taken from *How to Pass Graduate Psychometric Tests* by Mike Bryon, also published by Kogan Page.

ANSWERS TO TESTS

Spelling test, page 88

1. accommodation, 2. the effect (affect is a verb), 3. fulfil, 4. no error, 5. abysmally, 6. personnel, 7. guaranteed, 8. no error, 9. targeted, 10. the stationary car.

Use of English, page 88

1. A, 2. A, 3. C, 4. A (split infinitive), 5. A (contains a dangling participle phrase), 6. C, 7. A, 8. D, 9. B, 10. C.

Reasonable logic, page 90

1: A incorrect, B correct; 2: both incorrect; 3: A correct, B incorrect; 4: A incorrect, B correct.

Yet more logic, page 92

1. not possible to say, 2. not possible to say, 3. not possible to say, 4. true.

9

Frequently asked questions

Is it true that it's not what you know, but who you know?

Afraid so, yes. If you know the producer of a certain television show and want to work for it, you stand a better chance than if you do not know the producer. If you want to work as assistant camera operator on a film it is really not going to happen unless the camera operator knows you. There are two points to be made, however. First, you can get to know these people, and second, that is not the sole determinant of success. You still have to be able to deliver and do the job people want you to do. If you are fortunate enough to be the director's son or daughter, get work as a runner but behave as if menial work is way below you or generally annoy the people around you, everyone will avoid employing you in the future. (They might also think twice about employing your dad or mum if you are always part of the package.)

You can get to know the right people – it's not an exclusive club. Working in the media requires a lot of networking but this does not mean dressing up, putting on a show, making a bee-line for important people and getting in their face 24 hours a day. Casual conversations about shared interests or favourite programmes can be enough to get your name in the right person's head. Networking is just that, and the person you talk to might not be the person who employs you, but he or she might know someone who knows someone.

How much money will I earn?

1. Not a lot. Your first work is likely to be work experience and unpaid. There could well be no way around this, and you have to accept the debt you are going to get into. Your first job may take up every single working hour in the day and only pay £200 per week IF THAT. And don't forget that even if you become a successful film director, writer, columnist or broadcaster, you are by no means guaranteed a regular or high income. Indeed, some workers in the media simply don't care about this – such is their passion and belief in what they do that the financial side of the equation is not expected to add up.

2. Loads of moolah. You're gonna be a star, a celebrated director, writer and maybe even have your own television production company, and let's face it, if someone can get a million dollars for a single episode of a sitcom, why can't you? Senior managers of television companies – broadcasters and independent programme makers – earn over £100,000 per year. Write a fantastic book, launch a fantastic internet company and you'll make millions. You will revel in your wonderfully creative career and retire to your own personal tropical island while others wish they had started a pension scheme when they hit their eighteenth birthday.

3. An OK amount. It ends up being fairly comparable to other professions, except if you are freelance you will find you earn more per week on short-term contracts than full-time employees tend to earn per week. Hence, some magazine editors will be content with between £30–50,000 per year, television directors and producers will land upwards of £1,000 per week (unless budgets are really tight), and film directors will make sure their agent carves out a nice six-figure sum from the overall budget, plus a percentage of box-office take if they are feeling really bolshy and reckon the finished product will be a blockbuster.

What is/are media sales?

Flick through the media section of any jobs page and you will find more of these than any other job opportunity. As you might expect, these are sales jobs in the media. Unless you work for the BBC, the principal revenue for your employer is going to come from advertisers – private companies who want to get themselves in front of your viewers, readers or listeners. Media salespeople phone up potential clients and try to convince them to spend money with the media organisation. The job can be extremely stressful. Once you have made a sale against the medium, you then need to ensure the client delivers the advertising material to deadline, and that it is suitable to appear. And even when it has appeared there is the job of credit control – ensuring the advertiser actually pays up for the appearance. Depending on the medium and company you work for, you may or may not feel very much involved with the medium itself. Some trade magazines operate by getting the sales staff to talk to companies in their interest area, and allowing the companies to dictate the editorial content – but in any case the sales staff do need to know a lot about their area to be able to sell effectively. At the end of the day, however, you may have little or no influence on editorial content. That said, media sales is still an effective way into the industry, since for some companies a sales background will stand you in good stead for management and strategy roles.

Can I take career breaks?

If you are careful, yes you can. The thing about the media industry is that you will find work as long as you are visible and the work you do is good. If you disappear off the radar of media companies for too long you may have an uphill struggle to prove you are up to the job – even up to your former job – and that you do understand how the industry works and what the specific challenges and trends are within your chosen field. You may be fortunate enough to be employed by a large company with the capacity to give you a secondment for a number of months, or alternatively as a freelancer you can decide to just take time away. But try to sort out what will happen when you return before you go. Make sure people will be expecting to hear from you when you return. Why not try to combine your break with research for something when you return (perhaps travel journalism, a travel show, a new job or life direction show)?

Can I switch between media?

It depends on your job. If you are a website programmer working with new media it is unlikely you will ever direct your own television drama without deciding on a significant shift in working life and career direction. Certainly in the early part of your career it is important that you decide whether you want to work in print, broadcasting or new media, and aim directly for that industry. That way your employers will be sure where your interests lie, and you can concentrate on getting to know that industry and working out how you can contribute and work in it. It is possible to take 'bi-media' qualifications and courses covering both television and radio. Some broadcast organisations – BBC and Flextech – run both radio and television stations, and certainly if you are a journalist you may find yourself contributing to both media at once. Indeed, there is also a chance that if your news service includes a website your work will appear on that as well, so you may naturally need to be able to communicate across media to get a job in the first place.

As you get further in your career it will be increasingly difficult to switch medium. If you want to be an editor, your employer will look for specialist knowledge and clear experience in that specific medium rather than general all-round skill. In television there appears to be very little crossover between documentary filmmakers and those who make drama programmes. Again it is not an impossible switch to pull off, but the industry does favour people with specialisms. In addition, as your career progresses it is likely that your industry contacts will all come from a certain area of the media, and a certain sector of that medium, rather than diverse places.

Working for the media is always fantastically interesting, isn't it?

Some media workers will tell you that because you are working with current events, contemporary stories, and often trying to relay information as soon as it comes to hand, working in the media is never boring. However, there are technical aspects to the work which can be tiresome and an all-round drag. If you find yourself not looking forward to spotting typographic errors in a 180,000-word manuscript or re-editing a radio or television programme for the fiftieth time in a week it will be time for you to move on.

You need to have a lot of patience to see through some of the technical processes of media production. You may find some people you work with are infuriatingly meticulous, as they seek to ensure every aspect of their programme, web page, book, film or feature is correct. You may find yourself having to go over the same elements of a story over and over again just to ensure your audience understands where you are coming from. If you are working to an external client's specifications – in contract publishing or website creation, for example – there is always going to be a time when the client goes back on what it originally said it wanted, and you have to go back to the drawing board. In general, though, the fact is that if you are doing a job in the media that you really want to do, there will never be a day when you don't want to go to work.

10

Where to study

DO I NEED TO STUDY AT ALL?

Yes you do

For positions in publishing a degree is pretty much a prerequisite, regardless of the subject matter of that degree – it just shows your academic achievement. For roles dealing with rights and media law, you must study law in the first place so you understand the context in which entertainment and related laws operate.

For positions throughout broadcast media a degree is likely to be looked for by employers, and is certainly a requirement if you want to get into a management role fairly swiftly and without too much fuss or donkey work.

In journalism it is a good idea to have a vocational degree or qualification – although it is not absolutely necessary. Your degree could be on a subject related to what you are writing about, such as history, economics or English literature, then you can pick up the journalistic and writing skills you require later.

In new media you will need evidence of technical skills in order to carry out the job for which you are aiming. Some new media employers and employees suggest taking a more traditional media-related course, simply to give you a clear framework on which to hang your skills. For example, a good media studies course should expose you to important theories around communication, visual or audiovisual. This kind of knowledge will provide a clear basis on which you can set and develop your ideas.

No you don't

A lot of roles and jobs in the media are awarded to those who demonstrate the practical ability to deliver rather than the theoretical knowledge about why the media works. You might be very good at identifying precisely why a particular programme works – why a visual effect is good and why a film is satisfying to watch – but that does not necessarily mean you can make a good show yourself.

It is far better, then, to get stuck in with the industry, to circumnavigate all those interviews and application forms by knocking on a few doors and getting yourself work experience inside a production company or three. If you find you need to get some recognised qualifications, you will know precisely why you need those qualifications and how to get them. You might even be able to get your employer to fund your study.

While it is impossible to put precise figures on the number of courses now available that are somehow media-related, the fact is that there are currently more people training in the media than there are opportunities for those students. In some parts of the media industry you could even find that a college or university course does nothing but postpone your entry into the profession for a few years, and then means you are over-qualified for the opportunities that do exist.

The proliferation of media-related degrees and qualifications means that even if you do get qualified your employers may not regard the qualification as being a mark of ability. Media studies courses may be run by colleges and universities who recognise a popular course when they see one, and are more concerned with getting students through their doors than they are with ensuring teaching staff are experienced in the sector. The result? A practically useless degree.

IF YOU DO TAKE A COURSE

- Make sure there are vocational elements to the course.

- Make sure there is contact with the industry – whether through lecturers, tutors or work experience.

- Try taking a sandwich course – get out into the industry and apply your skills to the real world.

- Make sure the department where you are training has up-to-date equipment and up-to-date ideas. There is no point in training on IT or broadcast equipment that is no longer in use in the industry.

- Find out what past students are doing now. Are they employed, and importantly, are they employed in jobs they studied for? Is this course clearly a stepping-stone into the industry, or is it just there for people who are interested in the subject but want to work elsewhere?

- How much freedom will you have to create your own portfolio of work? You want to leave the course with clear practical evidence of your ability, not just a certificate.

Most importantly, there is now such a range of courses provided by colleges, universities and a whole host of other training organisations that you can take a course that appears to be fairly specialist in a subject area. You can combine a general media studies course with particular emphasis on new media, on 'time-based media', on scriptwriting, presenting, anything you like. Again, if you want to make sure you get something special from your studies – something that really will mark you out from the countless others in search of a first job in the media – do something that keys in precisely with your chosen area of work. The more specialist and dedicated you appear, the easier you will find it to apply for the job you want, and the more open employers will be to taking you on.

There is a comprehensive online resource for finding the perfect media-related course for you. It is jointly run by the BFI (British Film Industry) and Skillset, the Sector Skills Council for Audio Visual Industries, and has over 4,000 courses listed. You can find it at www.bfi.org.uk/media-courses.

Check out also the www.support4learning.org.uk website created by Higher Education and Research Opportunities (HERO) HERO Ltd, Rooms 206/207, 2nd Floor, Technopole, Kings Manor, Newcastle upon Tyne NE1 6PA, tel: 0191 227 3549. There are more useful links on its home page at www.hero.ac.uk.

WHAT KIND OF COURSE?

- National Vocational Qualifications (NVQs) are qualifications that recognise specific workplace skills rather than theoretical or class-based knowledge. They are available across a wide range of media-related subjects. NVQs can be awarded at entry level or up to level 5. City and Guilds (www.city-and-guilds.co.uk) now awards almost 50 per cent of NVQs.

- Higher National Certificates (HNCs) or Diplomas (HNDs) are undergraduate-level qualifications, usually equivalent to two years of university study. These are work-related, so bear more similarities to NVQs than to degrees. On completion of some HNDs and HNCs you can go on to qualify at degree level.

- Foundation courses are usually one-year courses which deliver the basic skills and knowledge ready for more detailed study of the subject. They may not actually give you a recognised qualification, but they do prepare you for further study or for entrance into the industry. With a completed foundation course you may be able to take a degree course without having to take A levels.

■ The term 'sandwich' can be applied to several different kinds of courses (although usually to degree level), and generally indicates that the course is structured in two or more parts with an amount of time – sometimes up to a year – free from study in the middle. During this time the student is expected to go and work in the industry. This is an excellent way to get both a qualification and clear industry experience by the time you complete your studies. Find out how much help is given to securing good and worthwhile placements – is it entirely your responsibility, or does the institution have good contacts with employers in the industry which you can exploit?

■ Bachelor of Arts (BA)/Bachelor of Science (BSc): these are degree courses which tend to last three years. A BSc is normally awarded for more technical or scientific work, and a BA for artistic/academic skills. Find out precisely what the mix is between theory and practical on these courses.

■ Master of Arts (MA)/Master of Science (MSc) are Master's-level courses, taken by those who have already completed a bachelor-level qualification (or as a four-year-plus course instead of a bachelor-level qualification). These may run for one or more years, providing students with the chance to study more in depth in their particular field. Master's degrees may be very structured and practical, leading to vocational qualifications, but they can also be research-driven and more free-form, requiring the students themselves to identify a subject of study and to ensure this is relevant to the outside world of work.

■ For technical and vocational skills you may find short courses are most suitable. There are day-long workshops for skills such as television presenting, screenwriting and so on. Alternatively you might give up a weekend to study editing or film making on a new piece of equipment. People tend to take these courses in order to address a specific need to add to their skills and talents. These courses may not result in a specific qualification, but you will have definite vocational skills you can immediately use.

■ The Open College Network (OCN) provides accreditation for adult learning. This can apply to courses of any length.

COMPUTER PACKAGES TO KNOW AND LEARN

Apple Macs tend to be the computers of preference for those working in the media. Knowledge of these computers is more important by far than familiarity with PCs, particularly for publishing and layout tasks. However, don't forget that since working in the media requires a lot of team work, creations such as websites and visual designs must be able to be shared across both PC and Mac computers. Therefore, as a worker in the industry you should be happy and ready to work with both types of technology; as a web designer or new media worker you must make sure your work is accessible and operates on both kinds of technology.

For examples of Apple technology and its use in the media go to www.apple.com/pro/.

These are some of the most widely used computer packages:

■ **QuarkXPress** is a desktop publishing tool which allows the user to design and lay out material for newspapers, books and magazines (plus advertisements, leaflets and other publishing requirements). See www.quark.com.

■ **Adobe Photoshop** is designed for the creation and manipulation of digital images and photographs. It is used to get images ready for printing on paper and for online publishing. See www.adobe.com.

■ **Adobe Illustrator** is another image management software tool, this time allowing the user to create images from scratch rather than manipulate pre-existing images. See www.adobe.com.

- **Avid** is an editing software program used for television programmes and feature films. This technology supports a technique known as 'non-linear' editing. With conventional film the editing process consisted of starting at the beginning of the film and working through scene by scene until the end. With a non-linear system you can access any part of the film at any time and work on the piece out of sequence. See www.avid.com.

- **Final Cut Pro** – as Avid, but running exclusively on Apple computers. See www.apple.com/finalcutpro/.

- **Sadie** is a range of products for use in the creation of audio material. It can be used for creating radio programmes or for production work on music CDs. See www.sadie.com.

- **Macromedia** – if you want to create cool websites it is likely you will need Macromedia software to help you. Products include Studio (web development), Director (for DVD/interactive CDs and websites), Flash (for creating interactive web content) and Dreamweaver (a website builder). See www.macromedia.com/software/.

MEDIA COURSES

Note that in the following listings some academic institutions offer courses and specialisations in media other than those for which they are listed. For example, the National Film and Television School is clearly for those two media, but universities such as Westminster, the London Institute and Salford run courses other than straight media studies or radio.

Media studies

All these courses have practical elements, but make sure you understand exactly how much, and what kind of practical work they include. Media studies is also a popular subject to combine with other cultural, language and even business topics. If you get the right blend now, you may find it easier to get into the part of the media you are particularly keen on.

Blackpool and The Fylde College, Central Blackpool Campus, Palatine Road, Blackpool, Lancashire FY1 4DW; tel: 01253 352 352; www.blackpool.ac.uk.

City University, Northampton Square, London EC1V 0HB; tel: 020 7040 5060; www.city.ac.uk.

De Montfort University, Faculty of Humanities, The Gateway, Leicester LE1 9BH; tel: 08459 45 46 47; www.dmu.ac.uk.

Goldsmiths, University of London, New Cross, London SE14 6NW; tel: 020 7919 7171; www.goldsmiths.ac.uk.

Hull College, School of Art and Design, Park Street Centre, Park Street, Hull HU2 8RR; tel: 01482 598 744; www.hull-college.ac.uk.

Kingston University, Cooper House, 40–46 Surbition Road, Kingston upon Thames, Surrey KT1 2HX; tel: 020 8547 2000; www.kingston.ac.uk.

Lancaster University, Bailrigg, Lancaster LA1 4YW; tel: 01524 65201; www.lancs.ac.uk.

Liverpool John Moores University, School of Media, Critical and Creative Arts, Dean Walters Building, St James Road, Liverpool L1 7BR; tel: 0151 231 5112; www.livjm.ac.uk.

London Institute (University of the Arts), 65 Davies Street, London W1K 5DA; tel: 020 7514 6216; www.arts.ac.uk.

Loughborough University, Loughborough, Leicestershire LE11 3TU; tel: 01509 263171; www.lboro.ac.uk.

Ravensbourne College of Design and Communication, Walden Road, Chislehurst, Kent BR7 5SN; tel: 020 8289 4900; www.ravensbourne.ac.uk.

Reigate School of Art, Design and Media, Media Division, Gatton Point North, Claremont Road, Redhill, Surrey RH1 2JX; tel: 01737 772611; www.esc.org.uk.

Royal Holloway, University of London, Egham, Surrey TW20 0EX; tel: 01784 434455; www.rhbnc.ac.uk.

University College London, Gower Street, London WC1E 6BT; tel: 020 7679 2000; www.ucl.ac.uk.

University of Central England, Perry Barr, Birmingham B42 2SU; tel: 0121 331 5595; www.uce.ac.uk.

University of Sheffield, Western Bank, Sheffield S10 2TN; tel: 0114 222 2000; www.shef.ac.uk.

University of Westminster (which recently came top in a *Guardian* newspaper listing of places to study Media studies), 309 Regent Street, London W1B 2UW; tel: 020 7911 5000; www.wmin.ac.uk.

Television

Again, this is a popular subject to mix in with other first-degree subjects. Also look out for MAs in specific television-related occupations such as writing and directing.

Bexley College, Tower Road, Belvedere, Kent DA17 6JA; tel: 01322 442 331; www.bexley.ac.uk.

South East Essex College, Carnarvon Road, Southend-on-Sea, Essex SS2 6LS; tel: 01702 220400; www.southend.ac.uk.

Stevenson College, Bankhead Avenue, Sighthill, Edinburgh EH11 4DE; tel: 0131 535 4700; www.stevenson.ac.uk.

Stockport College of Further and Higher Education, Wellington Road South, Stockport, Cheshire SK1 3UQ; tel: 0845 230 3102; www.stockport.ac.uk.

University of Bristol, Department of Drama, Cantocks Close, Woodland Road, Bristol BS8 1UP; tel: 0117 928 9000; www.bris.ac.uk.

University of Derby, Kedleston Road, Derby DE22 1GB; tel: 01332 590 500; www.derby.ac.uk.

University of Glamorgan, School of Electronics, Pontypridd CF37 1DL; tel: 0800 716 925; www.glam.ac.uk/soe.

University of Wales, Aberystwyth, Department of Theatre, Film and Television Studies, Parry-Williams Building, Penglais Campus, Aberystwyth SY23 2AJ; tel: 01970 622828; www.aber.ac.uk/tfts.

Film

Of all subject areas covered in this book, film is the least likely to have a full degree course dedicated solely to the practice and technique of creation. Courses on film are most likely to take an academic, analytical and critical angle on the subject, focusing on the study of directors and film genres or schools, how and why they exist, rather than what to do behind the lens. As such you will probably have to study film at undergraduate level as a combined subject, perhaps with a foreign language or another culturally based subject. This may not be an entirely bad thing, however, since films produced by other countries and continents can be truly inspiring for British practitioners. Moreover, the ability to demonstrate an awareness of foreign film and to speak a foreign language will stand you in good stead with industry employers.

That said, even if you read film studies at university you will have to undergo more industry or vocational specific training before you can actually carry out a proper job in the industry.

Aberdeen University, Student Recruitment and Admissions Service, University Office, King's College, Aberdeen AB24 3FX; tel: 01224 272090; www.abdn.ac.uk/sras.

Bolton Institute of Higher Education, Chadwick Campus, Chadwick Street, Bolton BL2 1JW; tel: 01204 528851; www.ase.bolton.ac.uk.

Queen's University Belfast, University Road, Belfast BT7 1NN; tel: 02890 245133; www.qub.ac.uk.

South Thames College, Media, Music and Performing Arts Programme Area, Wandsworth High Street, London SW18 2PP; tel: 020 8918 7777; www.south-thames.ac.uk.

Southampton Institute, Faculty of Media, Arts and Society, East Park Terrace, Southampton SO14 0YN; 023 8031 9000; www.solent.ac.uk.

University of Edinburgh, College of Humanities and Social Science, David Hume Tower, George Square, Edinburgh EH8 9JX; tel: 0131 650 4646; www.arts.ed.ac.uk.

University of Glasgow, Department of Theatre, Film and Television Studies, Gilmorehill Centre, Glasgow G12 8QQ; tel: 0141 330 3809; www.tfts.arts.gla.ac.uk.

University of Stirling, Department of Film and Media Studies, Stirling FK9 4LA; tel: 01786 467520; www-fms.stir.ac.uk.

University of the West of England, Bristol (UWE Bristol), Faculty of Humanities, Languages and Social Sciences, St

Matthias Campus, Oldbury, Court Road, Fishponds, Bristol BS16 2JP; tel: 0117 965 6261; www.uwe.ac.uk.

Radio

Again, those wishing to work in radio should also consider either a broadcast journalism course or a first degree in an alternative subject followed by clear vocational training on technical equipment.

Academy of Radio, Film and Television, American Building, 79A Tottenham Court Road, London W1T 4TD; tel: 020 8408 7158; www.media-courses.com (courses also available in Manchester, Dublin, Cardiff, Birmingham and Glasgow).

Bournemouth Media School, Bournemouth University, Talbot Campus, Fern Barrow, Poole, Dorset BH12 5BB; tel: 01202 524111; media.bournemouth.ac.uk.

City College Coventry, Tile Hill Lane, Tile Hill, Coventry CV4 9SU; tel: 024 7679 1000; www.covcollege.ac.uk.

Commedia Sheffield, Drum Media Centre, 6 Paternoster Row, Sheffield S1 2QQ; tel: 0114 281 4082; www.sheffieldlive.org.uk (age range from 13–24-year-olds with courses for the unemployed 16+).

East Surrey College, Journalism Department, Gatton Point North, Claremont Road, Redhill, Surrey RH1 2JX; tel: 01737 772611; www.esc.org.uk.

Edinburgh's Telford College, South Campus, Crewe Toll, Edinburgh EH4 2NZ; tel: 0131 332 2491; www. ed-coll.ac.uk.

Farnborough College of Technology, School of Media and Visual Arts, Boundary Road, Farnborough, Hampshire GU14 6SB; tel: 01252 407040; www.farn-ct.ac.uk.

Lambeth College, Vauxhall Centre, Belmore Street, Wandsworth Road, London SW8 2JY; tel: 020 7501 5000; www.lambethcollege.ac.uk.

Nottingham Trent University, Centre for Broadcasting and Journalism, Burton Street, Nottingham NG1 4BU; tel: 0115 848 5803; www.cbj.ntu.ac.uk.

South Kent College, Media Centre, Maison Dieu Road, Dover, Kent CT16 1DH; tel: 01304 244300; www.southkent.ac.uk.

Stroud College, Stratford Road, Stroud, Gloucestershire GL5 4AH; tel: 01453 761126; www.stroud.ac.uk.

University of Salford, Faculty of Arts, Media and Social Sciences, School of Media, Music and Performance, Adelphi, Peru Street, Salford, Manchester M3 6EQ; tel: 0161 295 5000; www.salford.ac.uk.

Publishing

You will find you can take any subject at degree level and still get into publishing. History, languages, legal degrees and of course English literature are always going to be the most relevant – or at least something from the arts side rather than science. It is possible to study publishing and printing at MA level, so again, if you are taking the education route, get a first degree in an arts-related subject and then go on to do an MA or diploma.

A science qualification could also be relevant if you want to get involved with the technical side of book making. The science of making and preserving paper, for example, may be viewed favourably by employers. See also listings under Industry Linked Training (below) for details on librarianship qualifications.

Abingdon and Witney College, Northcourt Road, Abingdon, Oxon OX14 1NN; tel: 01235 216212; www.abingdon-witney.ac.uk.

Blackburn College, Art and Design Curriculum Centre, Fielden Street, Blackburn, Lancashire BB2 1LH; tel: 01254 292929; www.blackburn.ac.uk.

City of Bath College, Avon Street, Bath BA1 1UP; tel: 01225 312 191; www.citybathcoll.ac.uk.

Community College, Shoreditch Campus, Falkirk Street, London N1 6HQ; tel: 020 7613 9123; www.comm-coll-hackney.ac.uk.

Leicester College, St Margaret's Campus, Grafton Place, St John Street, Leicester LE1 3WL; tel: 0116 224 2240; www.leicestercollege.ac.uk.

London College of Communication (LCC), London College of
Printing, Elephant and Castle, London SE1 6SB; tel: 020
7514 6562; www.lcptraining.co.uk.
Middlesbrough College, Faculty of Arts, Sports and
Recreation, Marton Campus, Marton Road, Middlesbrough,
Cleveland TS7 3RZ; tel: 01642 275000; www.mbro.ac.uk.
Northumberland College, Welbeck Building, College Road,
Ashington, Northumberland NE63 9RG; tel: 01670 841200;
www.northland.ac.uk.
Robert Gordon University, Schoolhill, Aberdeen AB10 1FR;
tel: 01224 262 000; www.rgu.ac.uk.

Journalism

Journalism can be studied through short courses, dedicated
degree courses, vocational courses and higher degrees at MA
and MSc level. Also look out for courses offering NCTJ recog-
nition – this shows the course is approved by the National
Council for the Training of Journalists (www.nctj.com; see
useful addresses).

Cardonald College, 690 Mosspark Drive, Glasgow G52 3AY;
tel: 0141 272 3333; www.cardonald.ac.uk.
City College, Brighton and Hove, Journalism Department,
Room 305 Pelham Tower, Pelham Street, Brighton, East
Sussex BN1 4FA; tel: 01273 667788; www.bricoltech.ac.uk.
Coleg Gwent, Pontypool and Usk Campus, Blaendare Road,
Pontypool, Gwent NP4 5YE; tel: 01495 333333;
www.gwent-tertiary.ac.uk.
East Surrey College, Journalism Department, Gatton Point
North, Claremont Road, Redhill, Surrey RH1 2JX; tel: 01737
772611; www.esc.org.uk.
Harlow College, Velizy Avenue, Harlow, Essex CM20 3LH;
tel: 01279 868000; www.harlow-college.ac.uk.
Napier University, School of Communication Arts, Craighouse
Road, Edinburgh EH10 5LG; tel: 0500 353570;
www.napier.ac.uk.
noSWeat Journalism Training, 25b Lloyd Baker Street,
London WC1X 9AT; tel: 020 7713 1000;
www.nosweatjt.co.uk.

Sheffield College, PO Box 345, Sheffield S2 2YY; tel: 0114 260 3603; my.sheffcol.ac.uk.
Sutton Coldfield College, Lichfield Road, Sutton Coldfield, West Midlands B74 2NW; tel: 0121 3362 1111; www.sutcol.ac.uk.
Wolverhampton College, Wulfrun Campus, Paget Road, Wolverhampton WV6 0DU; tel: 01902 836000; www.wolverhamptoncollege.ac.uk.

New media

If you wish to get involved in the programming side of new media, it is possible to get into the industry through training for computer programming skills alone. However, success in the industry – the attainment of leading positions – requires an amount of business knowledge and the ability to contribute to the ongoing direction of an organisation in its particular marketplace. You may be able to pick up this knowledge as you work in the industry but a qualification that enables you to learn more about the business and the uses of new media will give you a head start.

Again, be sure your course has plenty of practical work included, and if at all possible go for a course which includes work placements with successful new media companies.

Central Saint Martins College of Art and Design, Short Course Office, Southampton Row, London WC1B 4AP; tel: 020 7514 7000; www.csm.linst.ac.uk.
Falkirk College of Further and Higher Education, Grangemouth Road, Falkirk FK2 9AD; tel: 01324 403000; www.falkirkcollege.ac.uk.
Havering College of Further and Higher Education, Department of Art and Design, Harrow Lodge Campus, Hyland Way, Hornchurch, Essex RM11 1DY; tel: 01708 455011; www.havering-college.ac.uk.
London College of Music and Media, Thames Valley University, St Mary's Road, Ealing, London W5 5RF; tel: 0800 036 8888; www.tvu.ac.uk.

Tower Hamlets College, Creative Computing Section, Poplar Centre, Poplar High Street, London E14 0AF; tel: 020 7510 7777; www.tower.ac.uk.

University Centre Hastings, Havelock Road, Hastings, East Sussex TN34 1DQ; tel: 01273 877 888; www.sussex.ac.uk/cce.

University of Brighton, School of Computing, Mathematical and Information Sciences, Moulsecoomb, Brighton BN2 4GJ; tel: 01273 600900; www.brighton.ac.uk.

University of Leeds, Institute of Communications Studies, Leeds LS2 9JT; tel: 0113 243 1751; newmedia.leeds.ac.uk.

University of Luton, Department of Media Arts, 75 Castle Street, Luton, Bedfordshire LU1 3AJ; tel: 0800 389 66 33; www.luton.ac.uk.

University of Surrey Roehampton, Erasmus House, Roehampton Lane, London SW15 5PU; tel: 020 8392 3000; www.roehampton.ac.uk.

West Herts College, Creative Industries, Watford Campus, Hempstead Road, Watford, Hertfordshire WD17 3EZ; tel: 01923 812 525; www.westherts.ac.uk.

Westminster Kingsway College, Kentish Town Centre, 87 Holmes Road, London NW5 3AX; tel: 020 7556 8001; www.westking.ac.uk.

Industry-linked/commercial training bodies

These organisations deliver more vocational and professional skill courses. For commercially run training businesses you will need to find finance for courses yourself, so you must be certain the skills you will get are going to pay dividends.

BBC Training and Development (all aspects of media offered), Wood Norton, Evesham, Worcs WR11 4YB; tel: 0870 122 0216; www.bbctraining.com.

Chartered Institute of Library and Information Professionals (CILIP), 7 Ridgmount Street, London WC1E 7AE; tel: 020 7255 0500; www.cilip.org.uk.

Four Corners Film Workshop (television editing – for low income/unemployed), 113 Roman Road, Bethnal Green, London E2 0QN; tel: 020 8981 4243/6111.

FT2 – Film and Television Freelance Training, FT2, 4th Floor, Warwick House, 9 Warwick Street, London W1B 5LY; www.ft2.org.uk (contact via website or post only).

James Brice Associates (digital television skills), 2 Court Gardens, Stoodleigh, Tiverton, Devon EX16 9PL; tel: 01398 351515; www.jamesbrice.com.

Metro New Media, 35 Kingsland Road, Shoreditch, London E2 8AA; tel: 020 7729 9992; www.metronewmedia.com.

National Film and Television School (film and television, technical and creative training), Beaconsfield Studios, Station Road, Beaconsfield, Bucks HP9 1LG; tel: 01494 731425; www.nftsfilm-tv.ac.uk.

Northern Visions Media Centre, 4 Lower Donegall Street Place, Belfast BT1 2FN; tel: 02890 245495; www.northernvisions.org.

Phoenix Media Centre, Bradninch Place, Gandy Street, Exeter EX4 3LS; tel: 01392 667080; www.exeterphoenix.org.uk.

Raindance Ltd (lo-to-no budget film making), 81 Berwick Street, London W1F 8TW; tel: 020 7287 3833; www.raindance.co.uk.

SAE Institute, United House, North Road, London N7 9DP; 020 7609 2653; www.sae.edu (also delivers courses in Liverpool and Scotland).

Skillset (the Sector Skills Council for the Audio Visual Industries), Prospect House, 80–110 New Oxford Street, London WC1A 1HB; tel: 020 7520 5757; Skillsformedia helpline 08080 300900 (England), 0808 100 8094 (Scotland); www.skillset.org (recently started a new joint initiative with other industry bodies to establish a new entry training scheme for post-production staff).

Vivid (16 mm film making), Unit 311, The Big Peg, 120 Vyse Street, Birmingham B18 6ND; tel: 0121 233 4061; vivid.org.uk.

11

Useful addresses

A swift internet search will deliver the home pages for news-papers, magazines, books and most television stations complete with contact numbers and even careers/job pages and advice.

UNIONS, PROFESSIONAL ASSOCIATIONS AND INTEREST GROUPS

Association of British Science Writers, Wellcome Wolfson Building, 165 Queen's Gate, London SW7 5HE; tel: 0870 770 3361; www.absw.org.uk.

Association of Learned and Professional Society Publishers (ALPSP), South House, The Street, Clapham, Worthing, West Sussex BN13 3UU; tel: 01903 871 686; www.alpsp.org (the international trade association for not-for-profit publishers and those who work with them).

Association of Online Publishers, Queens House, 28 Kingsway, London WC2B 6JR; tel: 020 7400 7510; www.ukaop.org.uk.

Book Industry Communication, 39–41 North Road, London NY 9DP; tel: 020 7607 0021; www.bic.org.uk.

Bookseller's Association, 272 Vauxhall Bridge Road, London SW1V 1BA; tel: 020 7834 5477; www.booksellers.org.uk.

British Academy of Film and Television Arts (BAFTA), 195 Piccadilly, London W1J 9LN; tel: 020 7734 0022; www.bafta.org.

British Council Arts Group, 10 Spring Gardens, London SW1A 2BN; tel: 020 7389 3194; www.britishcouncil.org (also at The Tun, 3rd Floor, 4 Jackson's Entry, Holyrood Road, Edinburgh EH8 8PJ; tel: 0131 524 5714; 28 Park Place, Cardiff CF10 3QE; tel: 029 20 397 346).

British Film Institute, 21 Stephen Street, London W1T 1LN; tel: 020 7255 1444; www.bfi.org.uk.

British Interactive Media Association (BIMA), Briarlea House, Southend Road, South Green, Billericay CM11 2PR; tel: 01277 658107; www.bima.co.uk (the trade association representing the diverse interests of the UK interactive industry).

British Printing Industries Federation, Farringdon Point, 29–35 Farringdon Road, London EC1M 3JF; tel: 0870 240 4085; www.bpif.org.uk.

Broadcast Entertainment Cinematograph and Theatre Union (BECTU), 373–377 Clapham Road, London SW9 9BT; tel: 020 7346 0900; www.bectu.org.uk.

Broadcast Journalism Training Council, 18 Miller's Close, Rippingale, Nr. Bourne, Lincolnshire PE10 0TH; tel: 01778 440025; www.bjtc.org.uk.

Commercial Radio Companies Association, The Radiocentre, 77 Shaftesbury Avenue, London W1D 5DU; tel: 020 7306 2603; www.crca.co.uk.

Digital Media Centre, DIT, Aungier Street, Dublin 2, Eire; tel: 031 4023047; www.dmc.dit.ie.

Digital TV Group, 7 Old Lodge Place, St Margarets, Twickenham TW1 1RQ; fax: 020 8891 1999; www.dtg.org.uk.

Directors Guild of Great Britain, Acorn House, 314–320 Gray's Inn Road, London WC1X 8DP; tel: 020 7278 4343; www.dggb.co.uk.

Guild of Television Cameramen, Membership Secretary, April Cottage, The Chalks, Chew Magna, Bristol BS40 8SN; tel: 01822 614405; www.gtc.org.uk.

Literary Consultancy, 2nd Floor, c/o Diorama Arts, 34 Osnaburgh Street, London NW1 3ND; tel: 020 7 813 4330; www.literaryconsultancy.co.uk (will assess manuscripts for new authors).

National Council for the Training of Journalists, Latton Bush Centre, Southern Way, Harlow, Essex CM18 7BL; tel: 01279 430009; www.nctj.com.

National Union of Journalists, 308 Gray's Inn Road, London WC1X 8DP; tel: 020 7278 7916; www.nuj.org.uk.

Newspaper Society, Bloomsbury House, 74–77 Great Russell Street, London WC1B 3DA; tel: 020 7636 7014; www.news-papersoc.org.uk (website includes links to local, regional and national press).

Press Association, 292 Vauxhall Bridge Road, London SW1V 1AE; tel: 020 7963 7000; www.pa.press.net (also Northern Headquarters, Bridgegate, Howden, East Yorks DN14 7AE).

Professional Lighting and Sound Association (PLASA), 38 St Leonards Road, Eastbourne BN21 3UT; tel: 01323 410335; www.plasa.org.

Publishers Association, 29B Montague Street, London WC1B 5BW; tel: 020 7691 9191; www.publishers.org.uk.

Radio Academy, 5 Market Place, London W1W 8AE; tel: 020 7255 2010; www.radioacademy.org.

Scottish Press Association, One Central Quay, Glasgow G3 8DA; tel: 0870 830 6725; www.pa.press/scotland.

Sgrin, Media Agency for Wales, The Bank, 10 Mount Stuart Square, Cardiff Bay, Cardiff CF10 5EE; tel: 029 20 333300; www.sgrin.co.uk.

Skillset (the Sector Skills Council for the Audio Visual Industries), Prospect House, 80–110 New Oxford Street, London WC1A 1HB; tel: 020 7520 5757; www.skillset.org (loads of courses, careers information and links on the website; also see www.skillsformedia.com).

Student Radio Association, 5 Market Place, London W1W 8AE; tel: 07005 351999; www.studentradio.org.uk.

UK Film Council, 10 Little Portland Street, London W1W 7JG; tel: 020 7861 7861; www.ukfilmcouncil.org.uk.

Writer's Guild of Great Britain, 15 Britannia Street, London WC1X 9JN; tel: 020 7833 0777; www.writersguild.org.uk.

EMPLOYERS

BBC Broadcasting Centre, Portland Place, London W1A 1AA; www.bbc.co.uk (go to bbc.co.uk/jobs/ to find out about work experience and opportunities).

Channel 4 Television, 124 Horseferry Road, London SW1P 2TX; tel: 020 7306 8333; www.channel4.com.

Channel 5, 22 Long Acre, London WC2E 9LY; tel: 08457 050505; www.five.tv (recruitment: www.knw.com/group – the channel is owned by RTL, a European broadcast company).

Emap plc, 40 Bernard Street, London WC1N 1LW; tel: 020 7278 1452; www.emap.com.

Flextech Television, 160 Great Portland Street, London W1W 5QA; tel: 020 7299 5000; www.flextech.co.uk (cable and satellite broadcaster of LivingTV, Trouble, ftn and others).

Granada ITV1, Quay Street, Manchester M60 9EA; 0161 832 7211; www.granadatv.com.

Independent Television News, 200 Gray's Inn Road, London WC1X 8XZ; tel: 0207 833 3000; www.itn.co.uk.

IPC Media Ltd, King's Reach Tower, Stamford Street, London SE1 9LS; tel: 0870 4445000; www.ipc.co.uk.

ITV Network Centre, 200 Gray's Inn Road, London WC1X 8XZ; tel: 0207 843 8000; www.itv.com.

Penguin Books Ltd, 80 Strand, London WC2R 0RL; tel: 020 7010 3000; www.penguin.co.uk.

Random House, 20 Vauxhall Bridge Road, London SW1V 2SA; tel: 020 7840 8400; www.randomhouse.co.uk.

RTÉ, Montrose, Donnybrook, Dublin 4; www.rte.ie (and Fanum House, 108–110 Great Victoria Street, Belfast BT2 7BE; tel: 080232 326441; and branches around Ireland – see website listing at www.rte.ie/about/contact/nationwide.html. Ireland's public service broadcaster in television and radio).

Sky TV, Grant Way, Isleworth, Middlesex TW7 5QD; tel: 0870
240 3000; www.sky.com (or mail to Sky Resourcing, Human
Resources, BSkyB, Unit 3, Grant Way, Isleworth, Middlesex
TW7 5QD; e-mail: skyjobs@bskyb.com).

Ulster TV (UTV), Havelock House, Belfast BT7 1EB; tel: 02890
328122; www.utv.co.uk.

RECRUITMENT

The Bookseller, 5th Floor, Endeavour House, 189 Shaftesbury
Avenue, London WC2H 8TJ; tel: 020 7420 6000;
www.thebookseller.com.

Datascope, 109–110 Bolsover Street, London W1W 5NT; tel:
020 7580 6018; www.datascope.co.uk (recruitment agency
for games and new media).

Inspired Selection Limited Recruitment Consultants,
Clarendon Enterprise Centre, Belsyre Court, 57 Woodstock
Road, Oxford OX2 6HJ; tel: 01865 292 030; www.
inspiredselection.co.uk (publishing).

Mosaic Search and Selection Ltd Recruitment Consultants,
Kensington House, 33 Imperial Square, Cheltenham,
Gloucestershire GL50 1QZ; tel: 0870 7770896;
www.mosaicss.com (management-level appointments in
publishing, television and radio).

Recruit Media, Regency House, 1–4 Warwick Street,
Piccadilly, London W1R 5WB; tel: 0207 758 4550;
www.recruitmedia.co.uk.

Also available from Kogan Page

The A-Z of Careers and Jobs, 12th edn,
2005

Careers and Jobs in IT
David Yardley, 2004

Careers and Jobs in Nursing
Linda Nazarko, 2004

Careers and Jobs in the Police Service
Kim Clabby, 2004

Careers and Jobs in Travel and Tourism
Verité Reily Collins, 2004

Choosing Your Career, 2nd edn
Sally Longson, 2004

Great Answers to Tough Interview Questions, 6th edn
Martin Yate, 2005

How to Pass Numeracy Tests, 2nd edn
Harry Tolley and Ken Thomas, 2000

Readymade CVs, 3rd edn
Lynn Williams, 2004

Readymade Jobs Search Letters, 3rd edn
Lynn Williams, 2004

Test Your Own Aptitude
Jim Barrett

For these titles and more, visit the Kogan Page website at
www.kogan-page.co.uk

The above titles are available from all good bookshops. For further
information, please contact the publisher at the address below:

Kogan Page Limited
120 Pentonville Road
London N1 9JN
United Kingdom
Tel: 020 7278 0433
Fax: 020 7837 6348
www.kogan-page.co.uk

Index

account managers 77
accountants 68
actors 37
advertising 7–8, 41
animation 42
Apple computers 106
author 3, 14, 20–21, 37
Avid 61

BBC 2, 33, 35, 36, 43, 47–48,
  50–51, 59, 98
  Radio One 56–57
bookseller 27, 28
British Film Industry 104

camera operators 37, 60, 66
career breaks 97–98
catering 68
celebrity 3
CGI 60
content writers 75
convergence 72
copy-editor 22
corporate video 42
CV 29, 62, 79–80, 82–83, 86

director
  film 65–66
  of photography (DOP) 60
  television 38, 40–41

distribution 27–28
DJ 3, 48–49, 54, 56, 58
dot com, boom and bust 72

editorial assistant 22, 24–25
editors
  books 21–22
  film 66–67
  new media 75–76
  print media 11
  television 38

facilities house 38, 43
Final Cut Pro 61, 107

games industry 78

Harry Potter 2, 18–19

industry linked training bodies
  115–116
ITV 33

journalist 3, 5–8, 15–16
  freelance 12–13
  radio 52–53

lawyer, media 26–27
librarian 27
literary agent 26
location manager 60, 64

marketing   23, 79–80
media industry
  freelancers in   36
  sales   97
  size of   2–3
media studies   107–08
merchandising   68
money   96
music video   41

National Film and Television
  School   44
National Union of Journalist   15
Networking   62, 74–75, 81–82,
  85, 95–96

photographers   11
places to study
  film   109–111
  journalism   113–114
  media   108–109
  new media   114–115
  publishing   112–113
  radio   111
  television   109
programmers   76, 77–78
PR work   13, 26, 41, 68, 78
presenter   3, 38, 54
producer
  film   64–65
  radio   48–49, 53–54
  television   39–41
production
  assistants   37, 54

books   24
television companies   31, 36,
  45–46
publications
  book publishing   17–19
  contact publishing   8–9
  types of   6–7

reporters   10, 14
researchers   13, 37, 52
rights department   22–23
'runners'   62–63, 69–70

sandwich course   80, 105
scriptwriters   63–64, 103
sound recording   67
sub-editors   10, 22

technical crew   38, 54
television
  flexible workforce   32
  programmes   31–34

qualifications
  degree   101, 105
  foundation courses   104
  masters degree   105
  NVQs   104
  proliferation of   102
  vocational   101, 103, 104
Quark XPress   5, 106

web design agency   74–75